THE *Ultimate* RELATIONSHIP

...the one with yourself

Insights and epiphanies of a 21st century woman

FIONA PRICE

Cover photo by: Chris Ashley
Book design by: SWATT Books Ltd

Printed in the United Kingdom
First Printing, 2022

ISBN: 978-1-7396762-0-9 (Paperback)
ISBN: 978-1-7396762-1-6 (eBook)

Published by: Fiona Price
www.theultimaterelationship.co.uk

My wish, quite simply, is that my book adds inspiration to your journey.

Tracer

To my fellow women 'warriors'
who have the courage to live their truth

Readers' Plaudits

Fiona has untangled the how, why and where of being your own greatest support system, with razor-sharp honesty and self-introspection. Not a journey that many of us are brave enough to undertake. But with her support and words of wisdom, it becomes possible. That is why everyone needs to read this book. Not only is this a book to devour, but you can dip into it to find comfort and fortitude when weakened by everyday life. To have Fiona's experience and honesty is a godsend. Literally! – **Maria Wynne**

What a great title! Within minutes, I was engrossed and read the book in two days. Fiona offers amazing clarity about how to take charge of your life. I was lost, and her words rescued me. They helped me to understand the negative influences and thoughts that I had been unable to decipher. Therein lies Fiona's power and wisdom. Rather than hide, you have to face what makes you unhappy or seems confusing, and turn it into a tool which you can use to your advantage. – **Josey Evans**

Fiona's book is a poetic recognition that there is no path, no route map for us all to follow. Rather, our path is made by our own understanding. – **Mark Parkinson**

I cried reading this book because it rang such a deep toll within me. It also made me smile. This book will change the mindsets of so many women who feel that life is happening to them, not *for* them. It gives you the self-knowledge to change all of that. – **Deb Graham**

A pure delight for anyone with the ambition to live well, play hard and run a successful business. As a former athlete and a business owner myself, Fiona's anecdotes and insights resonated with me. There are daily actions we can all take based on her experience, which will help us live life to the fullest. Bring an open and curious mind to this book and wallow in the enlightenment. – **Andrea Sexton**

Having worked with Fiona in the past, I was keen to get my hands on this book. My only regret is that I wasn't brave enough to ask her about the concepts contained within, a decade ago. But as the saying goes, 'when the student is ready, the teacher will appear'. Fiona's background as an athlete and a successful business woman gives credibility to the principles contained in the book. She is living proof of the approach to life she writes about. – **Christina Jones**

Contents

Story Behind the Book 1

Mind of a Mentor 5

Poems 67

    15th Birthday   68
    Come Celebrate With Me   71
    Eventing Invocation   73
    Fanny's Poem   75
    Father Dear   78
    Hay Making Ode   80

Biz-Chat 83

    Women don't sell   84
    Truth in business   84
    Standing out from the crowd   85
    Good ideas   86
    Surround yourself with the right people   87
    The best you can be   88
    The power of change   90
    What is instinct?   91
    Working excessively   92
    Does success equal happiness?   92

Talks **95**

Introduction   96
'Stuff'   98
The ultimate relationship   108
Passion   119
How to network   122
Launching a new era   126
Feminising the financial world   129
Grand finale   133

Article **139**

Empowering the poorest women   140

Blogs **149**

A question of survival   150
Timing is everything   151
Secret lives   153
The path to freedom   156
What my animals have told me   159
Counting my blessings   162
Conflicted   164
Only I can fix me   166
Don't ask, don't get!   168
A love-hate relationship with the news   169
Our true human nature   172
What makes us who we are?   173
Silencing fear   174
A matter of life and death   177
Mirror, mirror?   179
A peculiar type of logic   181
The reincarnation of Lomax   183
It's all in the mind   185
Personal sacred space   189
The end?   192
Who am I?   194
Identity lost and found   197

A moment in time   198
Many lifetimes in one   200

Podcasts **203**

The power of thought   204
Narrating your life   206
Training your instinct   208
What is spirituality?   210
Talking to your food   212
Affirmations and how to change your life   214
How to take charge of your body and your health   217
How to regain your balance and equilibrium   221
How to help others using the power of thought   224
Consciously creating the life you want   226
Dowsing with a pendulum – the ultimate 'smart' device   230
Connecting with nature   233
Quantumness   237

Final Words **241**

About Fiona Price **243**

Story Behind the Book

For as long as I can remember I have been searching for answers to questions. Big ones such as the 'why, what and how' of all that there is and my role in it. And practical ones such as how to communicate with my body to create good health and repair it when it's broken, how to be more effective and how to create more of what I want in life.

In the process, I have learned that the ultimate relationship is the one with yourself. What you think and how you respond to every situation defines who you are and what you experience. Realising this is the easy part, living it is much harder.

The quest to change myself and the world around me led me to create businesses based on the things I was passionate about. My first long-term business (which began in 1988) was born out of a mission to help women become financially independent, an idea which was unheard of at the time. I also set up a non-profit organisation to promote women in the financial sector, who were an inspirational minority. Later on, in the pioneering days of video online, I set up a website to publish interviews with top UK businesswomen which showcased their different leadership style.

A subscription video website came next. This time, to inspire horse owners through providing insights into how top equestrians trained and cared for their equine athletes. And more recently, a website sharing my own 'rewilding' experience in Wales, including the trials and tribulations of living alone in a remote location. These businesses and others, plus my sporting endeavours, provided continual challenge and change which has been a catalyst for personal growth. And that brings me to this book.

When I was packing up to move from Wales in 2021, I decided it was time to say goodbye to several boxes of written material that I had carried around for years. They contained journals crammed full of thoughts, insights and epiphanies that had helped me make sense of my life, talks I had given, and articles, diaries and poems I had written. A bonfire beckoned but I felt compelled to read everything one last time. After I had done this, I still couldn't commit my writings to ashes without sharing the best of what had been so life-changing for me.

The Ultimate Relationship is an eclectic mix of my survival strategies for life, business and everything. It tells my story from the inside out through a bid to take control of my mind, my body, and my world. It also explains how I learned to hone my connection with the 'invisible helping hand' – that multi-dimensional part of us which will one day be explained by physics. The book is part narrative and part insight, woven into a guide to practical spirituality which, I hope, will help you to navigate difficult times and become a bigger, grander version of yourself.

We are at a turning point in history, which is a chance to reinvent our world. But we need to think and act differently. This requires a combination of the creative power of intuitive intelligence (a feminine attribute), harnessing our true power and a re-connection to the natural world. This, I believe, is the next evolution in human consciousness, which will enable us to step out of a 'problem-reaction-survival' mode, into something far more elegant. In so doing, we will change our lives.

Mind of a Mentor

This is a 'blog' that was written before the word blog was invented, in 2001, at a time where writing a journal about your life was still called a diary, when email was in its infancy and social media wasn't even a twinkle in anyone's eye. The internet was basic, few businesses had websites, and mobile phones were for speaking and texting only.

I wrote the diary for fun for a few months, after moving out of London. I was metamorphosing into another version of me in the lead-up to selling my business and was toying with the idea of writing a book based on a diary. But in reality, life was still too busy for this to happen.

Preamble

I seem to have acquired another job title to add to my list: 'Mentor'. It's a new direction for me and it's a new field, in its infancy, not yet a buzzword but it will be. The idea of mentoring isn't new. It's been around since time began, provided by friends, parents, teachers, siblings, colleagues etc. Let's face it, getting advice from the people around you is an accepted part of life.

In an age of the 'personal trainer' (for fitness, image, diet or anything else you care to imagine) some business and professional people are starting to recognise that objective advice about their life and career is a valuable, if not essential, support mechanism and, in some cases, it's survival. It's also not surprising, given growing work pressures and the increasing pace of life, that more people are also asking the question, "What is it all about anyway?"

As it happens, mentoring isn't new for me either. I've done it for as long as I can remember. I seem to draw people to me who need advice and guidance. And the truth is I enjoy it. There is little more pleasurable (except perhaps sex?) than being able to put your finger on the button for someone and reduce their mountain into a molehill, shatter the illusion of catastrophe and see the person catapult forward in consciousness. It has the 'wow' factor!

My theme for the moment (which came out of a poem I wrote for the co-directors of my business), is "We practise what we preach, we learn what we teach." This seems so true. I mentor myself (with the help of a few close friends and the odd book) and always seem to be learning what I am teaching. I'm inspired to impart what is current in my experience because that's what I can access most easily and feel most passionate about. Who I am, how I am, how my life is and what more I can be, are at the heart of everything I am and do. This is my personal quest, my search for truth, my search for happiness. This is at the very centre of my life, and it is what I try to offer others.

Even when I was a student, I knew my mission was to be a teacher and inspirer in the real-life, not classroom, sense. And for many years,

I felt I was betraying this by being in the financial sector. I wasn't, of course. I have been teaching all along – empowering women clients through providing them with an understanding of financial planning, as well as mentoring those I work with and others in the profession.

So, what lurks in the mind of a mentor? Come this way and you will see...

2nd May

Looking through cracks in the shrubbery at the end of my garden, I get glimpses of a vast sunset adorning my property (900 feet up a mountain). Uninterrupted views, however, have always been available from the other side of the fence, ie from the stable yard. Yes, the horses have the best seats in the house! Funny, I actually planned the stable yard for them to have magnificent views because to a horse a view is like a cinema screen – they see and sense so much more than we do, and it keeps them happy – very, very happy.

I recently took some photos of the sunset (between the gaps in the shrubbery). Studying these, I got the idea of lopping some branches off to make an arch and frame the view. By the time I saw my gardener, I had imagined the results from every upstairs room (mine is a house of many windows) and the plan had extended itself to taking down two whole trees.

Well, the result was breathtaking, absolutely breathtaking. The view is awesome, riveting, totally inspiring and has completely changed the way I feel about my home – I am really falling in love with it after nearly four years. Now, instead of thinking I may move in a couple of years, I am thinking about staying here longer and what else I will do with the place.

This was a highly symbolic act. The view had always been there – I just couldn't see it from the house and had accepted the inconvenience.

In a way, unveiling the view has allowed me to see several other wonderful opportunities in my life which have always been there, but were invisible. We have all the answers, if we can only find them.

One of my guiding beliefs is that we are capable, to a large extent, of determining what we experience in our lives. And if we don't exercise this power and practise the art of using it, then we mostly end up being a victim of seemingly random events unless, by chance, the coin flips in our favour. Where we are focused at any time is our point of attraction because 'like attracts like'. The beauty is that we can change what we get, by altering our focus and thus our point of attraction. So, we can create solutions. Solutions and problems are two sides of the same coin, like taking exams while knowing the answers already exist.

I had dinner tonight with a friend and he told me about various people who, over the years, had caused him grief. He had also recently lost several family members and a few friends, which always focuses the thinking and, in his case, the experience had started him on a Buddhist quest. So, the prominent thought in his mind was, "You have had countless lives before which means that everyone is your kind mother". Unsure that everyone around him had indeed been his kind mother, he nonetheless started to look for a glimmer of kindness in people – especially those who frustrated him. To his astonishment he not only found it but realised it had always been there. He was just seeing it for the first time. His attention to the negative aspects of his relationships in the past, had masked this truth.

12th May

Now that I have my 'view', I am frustrated to find I am drawn to an irritant at the bottom of the vista, instead of the magnificent cinematic horizon at the top. You see, the bottom edge has a line of leylandii trees which were planted in anger by my neighbours (with whom I have no communication). Unfortunately, they will, in time (and quite soon) obliterate my view. I live in the middle of nowhere and yet I have a neighbour on each side, which is a bit of a contradiction in terms, and a bit of a bummer!

However, I remember the law of attraction – my focus is my point of attraction. It goes something like this: "I get more of what I am focused on, whether I want it, like it, or not!" As far as the universe is concerned (the universe, in this instance, being an invisible co-conspirator which responds to the vibe you set on any subject), then if I am focused on something negative, I will get more of it and the more negative the focus, the quicker I will get it. No thanks! That's not for me. I am absolutely fascinated with how to create things in my life. Though I've not done a brilliant job historically, as life has been a bit haphazard, I am making better strides now that I understand the basic principles, and 'like-attracts-like' is a core one.

About the neighbours, I'll take you back a little because I can demonstrate what I am talking about here. We've had various run-ins (I won't bore you with the details) but suffice to say they involved the police, the local council, other neighbours and a great deal of harassment. It got out of hand and was very upsetting for a while. Although it's now resolved, in that verbal communication has ceased (despite efforts of reconciliation on my part such as Christmas cards, polite waves when they slowed down in their car for me when I was out riding etc), it reached heights of silliness when I found myself thinking I was being watched whenever I was outside (of course, I wasn't). I was also focused on them when I was driving down the lane to my house and could see their property next to mine, which gave me palpitations. Basically, I was far too aware of their presence for too much of the time.

I was even contemplating moving. Law of attraction at its worst, the result of escalating negativity and fear. Thankfully, I realised that moving wasn't the answer. Instead, I decided there must be an opportunity to learn something, probably about me. So, I needed an action plan. Step one, imagine said couple walking past my house (which they did several times a day) in clown outfits with big ginger hair, floppy shoes, flower in hats, and large red noses. Definitely not so scary. Possibly a little funny? Step two, repeat step one – often. Step three, remember that extreme behaviours, particularly aggressive ones, usually mask hurt and insecurity; I have seen it before. A bit more tricky when it's on your doorstep though. Step four, imagine said people feeling better about themselves, happy, smiling, pleased with life. Hold onto that thought every time I see them.

Something did happen and, as a result, things changed. I am not so aware of their presence and sometimes I don't even notice if they are in or out, or away for a few days. Best of all, I have stopped getting a panic attack every time I see them. The practical issues which caused the conflict in the first place have also subsided. Definitely an example of the 'inner game of tennis' – play stops if you don't hit the ball back. Energetically, by neutralising my emotional reaction to the triggers, there was no energy to be picked up by the other party. Powerful stuff. In fact, I can't even access the negative thoughts I used to have about them, anymore.

Back to the leylandiis. Anything is possible, even miracles, so if I don't focus on the trees and focus only on the exceptional view and enjoying it, the universe will conspire to deliver it to me. Maybe said leylandiis will suffer a case of spontaneous stunting? Anyway, I know it will be OK. A few days later, my weekend horse helper asked me if I was aware said neighbours had been overheard in the pub talking about moving abroad. Mustn't get too excited but yee-ha! My continuing focus will be on happy relations with my neighbours, whoever they are. I am the creator of my reality.

Later that evening, I walked into the kitchen at precisely the moment the lamp clicked on (it's on a timer switch). I love that. It happens a lot and I take it as a sign of the synchronicity of things.

20ᵗʰ May

Going showjumping with Clover Bay Leaf (aka Nicky) and Sam, whose new title is 'equine manager' as she doesn't like the term 'groom' – I can't blame her. Not the best of outings. Two mares in season, me and Nicky! Net result was uncoordinated on both parts, like some sort of unguided missile. Sadly, ended a good run of clear rounds on recent outings. Note to self – waste of time when hormones abound; in future, will aim to avoid such outings. Go for a pleasant ride instead, or just put feet up (yeah, right)! Better still, go shopping.

A further realization – showjumping doesn't suit my temperament, even on a good day, so will probably stick to eventing, dressage, and hunting (fox-free variety called 'blood-hounding' where you chase men runners instead, much better sport). I only went showjumping as a filler because eventing, which would be in full swing by now, has been cancelled due to the Foot and Mouth outbreak.

Problem with showjumping is all the waiting around and posing, neither of which I am good at. You have to estimate (from the number of entries) how long your class will take.

Usually, I do two classes and aim to put my number down to jump at the end of one class and the beginning of the other. This time, I badly underestimated the length of classes and ended up having to wait two hours before jumping in the first class and another two hours for the second, in boiling hot weather with the dog stuck in the lorry (new Foot and Mouth rules). All the time thinking about office work waiting to be done at home and housework too.

Should take a leaf out of Sam's book. Surrender to the moment, basically, chill out! Conversely, with eventing and dressage competitions, you get a drawn order, so you know exactly what time you will strut your stuff and can arrive and warm-up accordingly. Efficient, no time wasted. Much more me. So, I need to accept the fact that it is more difficult to change aspects of my temperament and play to my strengths.

On the way home, assumed role of agony aunt to Sam who is dealing with personal relationship issues. She's finally sorting her life out, which is great. I'm really pleased for her. Talked about focusing on the 'end place' of the change she wants to make, what it will feel like when she gets there, not how it will happen. If you focus on the desired result, the universe (divine intervention) will work out the detail and instinct will guide you there.

Funny how her stuff and mine, around relationships, coincides. Must be a bit like women working together who get synchronised menstrual cycles. Certainly happens at the office when the toilets have a habit of blocking at a particular time of the month. Yuck! Guess who has to clean them out? The boss, of course.

Ten past midnight, time for bed. Got to get up early to write a business mentoring Q&A piece for a financial newspaper before taking Ollie (proper name Aeolus, which is Greek for 'God of the Winds' – in your dreams, Ollie!) to a dressage competition. I like the seamlessness of life, working from home for a few days a week. Will ask for divine inspiration to wake up with ideas for the piece, which will save time.

Fall asleep to the sound of lambs bleating (healthy, Foot and Mouth free lambs) in the field next door.

21st May

Knackered but compelled to write another entry. This journal is becoming addictive, and I've only been at it a short while. Maybe it's purging, like a confessional?

Got up early and managed to write the piece in 45 minutes. Pre-sleep instruction worked. Didn't receive a real-life question for the column this time, so made one up about a person daunted by giving a talk. Remembered useful expression, 'The art of spontaneity is great preparation', very relevant. But the most powerful tool I have come across to stem nerves (before a talk, TV or radio interview) is to remember I'm there for the benefit of the audience, to provide them with information and clarity – that is my mission. For me, it's added pressure when I am called a 'financial expert' as I don't feel like one, but I am more expert than the audience, that is true.

Nerves are a performance-related thing, a function of ego which indicates the focus is back to front, ie self first. The reward (which is the 'self' bit) is feeling great afterwards. Had this epiphany when waiting to do a live interview on ITN *News At 10* and was panicking. Worked it out just in time, so the waiting was a gift.

Got away in the lorry with Ollie and his trainer Heather at 10am. He's too good a horse for me to compete in pure dressage. Dilemma is, I bought him to event and he's better at dressage which isn't my thing at all. Still, 'pick a thought' - I'm learning loads watching him being trained and competed by a professional, which will stand me in good stead for the dressage phase of eventing.

An illuminating day and a fabulously sunny one too. Lots of time to think. Ollie scored amongst the best marks in both classes and was placed in one, gaining six dressage points, so a good outing. He has had points in each of the three competitions so far and is still a baby in horse terms, age six.

Decisions, decisions! Resolved that Ollie probably won't event to a great level because of his showjumping. Eventing is a combination sport consisting of dressage, showjumping and cross country jumping – the latter over big, fixed, scary fences which is obviously the bit I enjoy the most. It's utterly exhilarating! Ollie has a strong inclination to please but thinks as long as he gets to the other side of the show jumps, it's irrelevant whether the poles stay up or not. Wrong, Ollie! W-R-O-N-G! I will probably persevere for a bit with showjumping and ask an expert for help but resolved not to push against the grain, if the grain doesn't want to go that way.

Only one snag, my fabulous eventing mare Clover Bay Leaf (Nicky) is going to have a baby by a gorgeous French stallion, so I won't have a horse to event and as I'm passionate about the sport, that won't do. Will have to get another steed... equals four horses, two cats and a dog called Benjamin. Convince myself it won't be overdoing it, as must be able to have an outing each week with at least one horse – whether hunting, eventing or dressage. Also, horses, like people get ill, tired and injured, so three horses in work is a good number. Hell, some have a nanny, I have a groom!

9pm and still at computer with a large bowl of ice-cream (organic, of course). Must hurry and finish as still got to get horses in from field and put them to bed (groom doesn't cover evening duties). Then have ritual candle-lit bath and turn in myself. 5am start tomorrow for London. Been coping well on less sleep recently (five to six hours a night). Tell myself that whatever amount of time I have to sleep, is the right amount for perfect rest.

Quickly check emails. Ten to deal with, including one from a producer at the BBC who interviewed me for a Radio 4 programme on people who have made dramatic changes to their work-life balance. Subsequently, I sent an idea for a series of dialogues with top businesswomen. Was referred to someone else and they have responded saying could be interested if I flesh it out a bit. I'm not thrown. Well, perhaps a bit. Thoughts for an inspired proposal needed quickly. Will think about it on the train to London tomorrow, if I can stay awake.

23rd May

Back home now and despite good intentions, slept blissfully all the way to London, so must think about BBC proposal today. Lots happening – patio being built so cement mixer grinding outside, garden being prepared for a makeover which equals noise and Sam on the tractor harrowing riding arena with a new harrow that isn't working well – more noise; local carpenter coming to discuss screens he's making for window seats (instead of curtains) in a moment, too. Must arrange MOT and service for horsebox and get stuck into work.

Will have to squeeze in a ride this afternoon, as Nicky and I need to practise dreaded dressage for our first horse trials of the year at Longleat next weekend. Visitors staying this weekend for bank holiday, so beds to make and cooking. Just a normal day. But fab weather, so all is well.

London was ballistic, a world of its own and alien to the rest of existence but you only discover this when you are no longer there full-time. For me, anything up to ten meetings a day is usual, yesterday only seven. I love the fast slipstream of activity though, intense problem-solving and decision-making, staying focused on the issues at hand, getting input from everyone involved and narrowing things down to a result that will lead to action. In some cases, further discussion is required but as long as clarity is gained about the issues of the moment and next actions decided, I consider that a result.

Yesterday, we finalised the recruitment of two Business Studies placement students on a sandwich degree course. One is very numerate and will work with our financial controller and the other will be the 'glue' at the bottom end of the organisation to answer phones, greet clients, make sure everyone has what they need, basically, the oil in the engine. Conversely, I think of myself as the 'glue' at the top end. I don't have direct responsibilities as I am a part-timer now. Instead, I have the luxury of being co-ordinator in chief and business guardian. Of course, I still carry all the financial risk but I own the majority of the business, so I guess that's fair.

We have had seven placement students over the years from various universities and I interviewed the latest batch at the University of the West of England last week. It is such an honour to interview bright, enthusiastic, untarnished youngsters who have their whole life in front of them. I always leave feeling inspired, wanting to take on several instead of one, so having two this time is good going. This is the first time we have been able to take on two, as they are salaried positions.

The directors' meeting was energized and inspired. I love working with these people and all my staff, in fact. Two of the three directors have worked their way up through the organization and been brought into the detailed running of the business in the last couple of years. They have really blossomed and it's great to see them as equals in terms of their ideas and ability to run things. The third joined last autumn and brings outside-the-box thinking. It feels like such a transformation from the past when there were lots of 'loose cannons' firing off in different directions. Still, that experience is part of how we are where we are now, so I'm grateful.

It was painful at the time as it meant losing some people but now we have a staff of thirty-five and rising, who are lined up and pointing in the same direction, and it is a joy. I learned it's virtually impossible to move an organization forward if people aren't coming at it from the same place. It takes enough energy to create momentum when they are. It's a nightmare when they aren't!

Various dilemmas presented during the day, such as changing job specs and the impact on the people concerned and the need to put a hold on recruitment to consolidate recent changes. Over the last eighteen months, we have re-invented the business with a 'blank sheet' approach. After twelve years, it seemed like a good time to ask ourselves, "How would we like to be in a world without limits?"

Participation came from all members of the company, and we found the courage to let go of a few previous ways of working. Have created something new and are proud of that. Moved to new premises (twice the size) to give us growing room – scary, as increases property costs from £60K a year to nearly £200K and spent a whopping £100K moving as well! Funded ourselves, with a little help from the bank – well, quite a lot of help, really.

During the 'blank sheet' process, we came up with three core objectives for the business which are: to be amongst the *best of the best* in our sector (we are generally considered to be so but there is always plenty more to do and no reason to be complacent); to provide the best possible environment for our staff (essential for a small business, actually a business of any size if you are going to keep people and fulfil your long-term promises to clients); and thirdly, to make a profit. All are equally weighted. The last bit seems to be a joke, oddly enough. A few weeks ago, I gave a talk about the changes we had made, and the audience laughed when I came to our core objectives. How sad that the equal weighting thing is so rare as to be laughable. Ironically, we have had insufficient focus on profit in the past!

At the directors' meeting, also discussed strategic ideas for growing the business in the next 3 to 5 years. Co-directors are now shareholders. It has taken a while to get my head around this psychologically and find the right source of advice to include them in the ownership – nightmare finding good advisers, as always. People are either tax advisers or business advisers, rarely both.

One of the great attributes of running your own business (also challenging) is that you make up the rules as you go along. Every day brings something new. I admit I have had the odd moment wondering what it would be like to work at a senior level in a big organization, spending other people's money?! But I wouldn't swap the experience. I knew when I came out of Business School at the age of 23, that I was unemployable. The MBA was overrated (as was a psychology degree before it) but it was a ticket to London to further my rowing ambitions. The MBA was geared to corporate life, no mention of being an entrepreneur. The only plus was learning the former wasn't for me. Basically, I wanted to be in charge of my experience, not part of a huge, inflexible, unwieldy, amorphous, corporate mass.

The risks, the uncertainty, the sleepless nights and leaps of faith were worth it, absolutely! I am who I am because of it all. And I believe I can do pretty much anything I choose, having had this experience and so much personal growth – from sport, as well as business. More to the point, I am following my heart and doing what makes me happy in my life and that is a blessing.

24th May

When I was younger I may have outwardly looked successful (bicycle to BMW 6 Series in one easy go) but I remember my then flatmate asking me if I was happy. I was dumbstruck. It was probably the first time I had ever thought about what 'happy' was and, in truth, I didn't know. And you can't change something until you are aware of what's missing. So, this question launched a period of great contemplation and introspection. Much unhappiness later, the answer is YES! I can safely say that I am happy (most of the time).

Happiness is that feeling of being in a pure, positive slipstream of energy which contains you, envelopes you, flows through you and over you; it's a feeling of peace and connection, the world going with you, and of infinite possibilities. It's a state of love and compassion where negativity doesn't exist. It's like a drug and I want more of it!

25th May

Last week, in a company meeting for all our staff (a quarterly event), I took the opportunity to share the 'feeling place' of our future plans. Talked about buzzing, happy people filling the building, creative and expansive energy, positive focus, debt-free, admired, fulfilled organization (staff, directors and clients). In short, optimum creative experience. It went down quite well. I have learned that creation starts with the 'feeling place', not a detailed list. Next step is to energise it by fantasising about it, then stay tuned for synchronicities which lead to information and opportunities. Finally, detailed action. Basically, instinct first, intellect second, the opposite of what is taught. Actually, we are not taught about instinct in our education system at all (especially business education), as the system only values intellect.

Went through history of the company too – funny stories about previous premises for the benefit of newer staff, to explain how yesterday's dream can become today's reality and today's dream can be tomorrow's reality. Funny to think back to our first offices in 1988, two small converted piano practice rooms over the Wigmore Hall. We were early adopters of new technology, with a fax machine and a word processor (basically, an advanced typewriter) – can you believe?! Had pine slabs for desks, stuck down on second-hand, two-drawer filing cabinets, and an area screened off for reception with a kettle on the floor which frequently looked like it was boiling up the skirts of our female clients, though no-one ever complained. Perhaps they were too polite? The things you get away with when you are a young start-up, or is it 'up-start', and it's your norm.

Same day, a meeting with the dreaded bank. A while ago, we extended our overdraft to assist with moving costs, expansion etc and, predictably, the bank insisted on a 'belt and braces' job (technical term), ie personal guarantee and a debenture which is a first call on business assets or revenue, in the case of default. Now, they also want a second charge on my property! I refused. Pees me off that all businesses, except for banks, accept an element of risk. I've never been frightened of banks, especially when asking for money. It's a two-way thing: they charge a *lot*, so I have the right to interview them for the job and negotiate terms. I told this to the very nice bank manager (our fourth in less than 4 years). I also told him I was hacked off with poor service and was considering moving elsewhere. So, it's up to him to make a gesture. Hate borrowing money and intend to pay it off asap.

27ᵗʰ May

Working at home. Working on a weekend is part of seamless living. The name of the day is irrelevant. Keep gravitating to the window to see different hues of the sunset. A spectacle I hate to miss. Nothing more beautiful than living art! How could anyone be tempted to watch the box when there is this to see, though I suppose most people don't live on the top of a hill. Just got back from my sister's where we had supper in the garden. They (sister, husband and three boys) live at same height on other side of valley, so we could almost send smoke signals. But I have open views whilst they are surrounded by woodland.

Their house is in the process of reconstruction, so it's a building site right now. They aren't living in it, they moved out while work is being done but like to visit it to remind the children where home is. While looking for a house to rent, they lived with me for a month and moved out days before my sis' gave birth to her third child, in a birthing pool. I coped well being overrun by a whole family, I think, especially as I have perfectionist tendencies. But spent quite a lot of time rubbing marks off the walls afterwards.

Finally, resolved that I am not interested in having children, lovely as they are for extremely short periods (half an hour, or so). Of course, this could change when I meet the right man – only joking! Sis' cooked pancakes on her Aga (surrounded by dust and plaster) as it was the birthday of one of her boys. She's a star, an enlightened mum, also a clinical psychologist and healer. I love her. As children, we quarrelled but now it's mutual respect, appreciation and love. Better than could have expected.

Discovered my dog Benjamin is a football star. The boys had to work hard to get the ball off him; he dribbled, marked and performed headers with great skill. I will have to buy him a football to go with the growing collection of other toys that lie around the place. Spoiled pooch! Benje is a stunning black and tan Jack Russell who looks like he is made from one perfectly formed and continuous muscle. He's lean, athletic and it's poetry in motion watching him run, twist and turn. You know what they say about dogs resembling their owners – here's hoping!

But funny how male animals grow into their sex organs! 18 months old and hormones have kicked in. Yesterday, he was found one mile down the lane dodging traffic on the main road – after a bitch on heat. Rescued in the nick of time by people who live down the lane, who bundled him into their car and returned him to me. The psychic protection I put around him obviously worked! I think he scared himself sufficiently that he won't go again. Benje is such a happy little chap. I only have to look at him to be reminded what happiness feels like, when I lapse. My animals are my family, and they are such good teachers.

As I was putting the car away when I got back from my sister's, I heard horses galloping around the paddock. Turned out to be two male horses fighting over the mare who was in season – more hormones flying around. A clairvoyant told me Ollie was in his first incarnation as a horse. Hadn't been in close quarters with a mare before (didn't really know one end from the other). Now, he's acting like a stallion but can't deliver as he doesn't have the equipment but he's seeing the other gelding off who is much bigger than him. Watched them strutting around for a while, a grand sight. Ollie, with tail high, flaring nostrils, dancing. Nicky, behind him at full tilt, kicking her heels (tart!) and big boy Harry, nose in the air, heading off in the opposite direction. Sun setting, birds tweeting, lambs bleating...

Idyllic scene spoilt by a call from Sam's mother (at 11pm) to say Sam's just split up with her man and has to move out of his flat tomorrow. Good for Sam, I encouraged her to do something to relieve her unhappiness. But inconvenient for me as she won't be in to work and it's too late to get help with the horses. In fairness, Sam (groom) has worked for over a year and never failed to show up through sickness, snow, accident and ice. She hasn't taken any time off except bank hols (her choice as opted for extra pay).

So, tomorrow I'll have to do the yard (muck out, hay nets, feed, water, sweep up, turn out) and exercise two horses. Had a mega day planned for work, food shopping, cooking for guests coming to stay, taking the pink horsebox (Lady Penelope) for a quote to re-spray so won't be the butt of rude jokes anymore, and taking Ollie to the gallops for fitness work before Longleat horse trials (both he and Nicky are entered). Won't make the gallops but most of the rest will have to be done. Sleep, what's that?

28th May

Deep breath and braced for the day. On the yard at the crack of dawn to feed and turn out. Dashed inside between riding two horses and yard chores to take phone calls and respond to emails. Good news on office dilapidations (cost of putting the offices we vacated back into good order) which have been negotiated down from £35,000 to £20,000. Still think it's daylight robbery but it pays to take professional advice. Next step, appeal against vast amount of rates we are paying on new premises. "A woman's work is never done" as my mother used to say.

Plucked up courage to email man at the BBC about the dialogue series, to let him know I'll get a treatment to him by the end of next week. Only problem, huge list of other urgent items for next week too. Will visualise an efficient week, achieving all with ease.

Can hear dog making muffled woofing noises in his dreams while he naps downstairs. Probably chasing rabbits or sniffing a pretty bitch somewhere. A phone call confirms that for a large amount of money, Lady Penelope (pink horsebox) can regain her respect by metamorphosing into a blue dragon.

Cooked monster fish pie, lush chocolate cake, Bakewell pie and cauliflower cheese for guests coming tomorrow, even though planning to also eat out (must be the Jewish mama in me!). New friend, D, coming with her two young daughters. D and I have masses in common. Met through business a few months ago at her office and within five minutes had barricaded the door, taken off shoes and were doing healing on each other. She runs a similar size business to mine, is equestrian, comes from the same background and is interested in everything alternative.

One of her many skills is that of a medical intuitive. She can look at you and tell you what's wrong medically. She saw a problem with one of my eyes when we first met, which was later confirmed by an optician. It shocked her, not me, that she was so accurate. I'm accustomed to this sort of thing as I trained as a healer myself and have a number of what others might called 'weird' friends. Will be a riveting few days, especially as I live in a very old house (originally listed in the Doomsday Book) and she may well pick up past inhabitants and other goings-on. Another clairvoyant friend picked up some very interesting stuff (or should I say 'spooks') last time she stayed.

5pm – debrief patio crew. It's nearly finished and looking fab. It was a risk using stone slabs because small samples can be misleading but the flagstones look terrific. Waiting for wicker hurdles to enclose the sides now, beautiful old-fashioned woven fencing.

As patio team disappears, unscheduled visitor, *Local Lover (LL)* arrives – mmmn! I've known him for a while (probably most of the time I've been here, so about three and a half years) but only been acquainted with 'he who is unavailable' on a more personal level for about a year, just after I ejected 'dearly betrothed' from my home and my life, which is a long story. I am generally principled about this sort of thing so took some persuasion to get involved but buckled under his charms in the end and bought the chat-up line that he and his partner (who are childless) lead separate lives, yeah right! Can't imagine it will end well but right now, it's beautiful and fits in with a life of perpetual motion.

Though we live in completely different worlds, I have to admit that I am very fond of *Local Lover* who constantly surprises me with his sharp wit and wisdom. If things were different, I could see myself in a relationship with him, but he is too frightened to make the leap and I have resolved not to hold it against him. I have learned through other relationships, that it is not for me to change him. If I agree to see him, it's because I want to, and I can change my mind at any time. And he knows that when I meet someone else, who is available... it's curtains.

Great loving it must be said, best to date and I'm grateful to *Local Lover* for the tremendous gift he has given me regards the growing connection with my sexuality, femininity and womanhood. Sensuality is such an important part of sex, and he is Mr Sensual! I feel like the cat that got the cream. Afternoon delight. Oh joy!

Really, really tired now. Long day and I am burning the midnight oil again. Just need to write a note for equine manager Sam about what the horses are doing tomorrow, then it's bed. Aiming for a lie-in.

Uncharacteristically, woke up at 5am, in need of water. Went down to kitchen to find the Aga perilously close to the danger zone. Had turned it up for mega cooking session and forgotten to put it back down again. Marvel at how my subconscious found a way to get me out of bed to sort it out. I always intend for safety in my life, so I know I am guided, zig-zagging through the perils of everyday existence.

1st June

So much has gone on in the last few days during D's visit. An illuminating, mind-blowing time from a number of perspectives. It felt strange with the house overrun by two young girls – bright, vocal, delightful and utterly demanding (as children of 2 and 5 usually are). But pleased I managed to retain a balanced state of mind despite continual rounds of feeding and playing games. Doesn't change my current perspective of not wanting children. Grown totally accustomed to personal space and lifestyle. Horses, dogs and cats are my constant companions and responsibility. Then there's the business and all my staff and clients. Children? Can't even go there. Life-changing in a way I do not find appealing. But hey, anything can happen.

Flux about children is a bit like relationships – always thought I would find a good one to last a lifetime. But currently think a relationship lasts as long as it's good – and that's it. Chances are, that isn't a lifetime (particularly as I am programming myself to live to an extraordinarily ripe old age, well past 100, without becoming decrepit). I'm sure age is a state of mind as I know we can influence our bodies. I am constantly being told I don't look anything like my age (41), so at this rate long life is a real prospect.

During D's stay, I made a number of important decisions concerning the horses. This was prompted by a conversation with D that tapped into the edges of my awareness but hadn't previously translated into conscious thought. First, dear Ollie will be sold. Thoroughly wonderful as he is, the truth is, we are not compatible. Unlikely his showjumping will improve and realistically, he is 'too much horse' for me (having matured physically in the year I've had him). He rides big and powerful, and I now find him harder work than I would like, even though I am strong for my small stature. Will find a loving dressage or hunting home for him and buy a good eventing prospect that can hunt a bit too.

Hate the idea of selling him. I never buy with an intention to sell, as I see myself as guardian and friend to my animals rather than owner. But there has to be something on both sides to make it work and he is young enough to have a great life elsewhere – he deserves the right connection with another rider. I believe there is a special person for every horse.

Leads me to my second decision. Been really peed off (should know better) that given the amount of time, effort and money I put into my wonderful horses, that I am not a better rider. I know I'm brave – my idea of fun is galloping to a 6-foot hedge out hunting with an unknown hazard (stream, ditch or drop) on landing or take-off, in the middle of a pack of other horses all doing 'Charge of the Light Brigade'; or tackling a large cross-country course when eventing. But at best, I have only been able to think of myself as an intuitive rider, with strength and balance acquired from my rowing days, rather than a good rider, in the technical sense. In fact, I have thought of myself as C-R-A-P on occasions.

D reminded me that I need a dream in order to focus my efforts; then must work on low self-esteem as a rider, and she's right. New resolve. I am going to aim for Advanced level at Eventing. Can 'taste' Intermediate level just round the corner, so Advanced will be my dream. Will talk myself up, not down, in future.

Why shouldn't I do it? There are worse riders who, with decent horsepower, have achieved great things. I can't change the shape of my body, but I can learn to carry it with poise and use positive imagery to improve. I wasn't the right shape for rowing either (too small) but represented my country many times and made it to the Commonwealth Games. So, I C-A-N do it. Yes, I can! Must align myself with new vision – really, really believe it's possible and expect divine intervention to help me with horse power, training and competition performance. That feels better. Now, I'm excited.

Decision number three, Nicky will be put in foal as quickly as possible. Will ditch the rest of the eventing season and face the fact that while she is the ultimate jumping machine and we have a 'poetic' partnership in that department, she isn't going to make the dressage – she just doesn't see the point – like Ollie doesn't see the point of showjumping. Grrhh! I wish I could combine their talents into one horse.

On the subject of babies (four legged ones), D is the third friend with psychic abilities to talk to my animals. As with others before her, she told me Nicky is gagging to have babies – the first thing Nicky 'said' to D was "Oh you're a mum, what's it like?" So, I'm going to go with the flow on this one.

On a different subject, she said my house is a portal to another dimension. D is not the first to say that either! She was sleeping in oldest room and picked up a load of other-worldly types who had lined up to talk to her. I acted as interrogator while she communed with them. Very interesting and great fun. Lots of mind-blowing information but that's another story.

I did a healing on D's children who responded with dramatic improvement virtually immediately which was pretty astonishing, and D did a healing on some psoriasis on my ears which improved remarkably by the next day. We generally mused over life and the universe together. We all had lunch with my sister, brother-in-law and two nephews in my favourite bohemian restaurant in the back of beyond, just down the road.

Benje was unstoppable, played with the kids during their whole stay. After they left, we crashed out (Benje and me) for several hours, before being able to resume normal duties.

2nd June

Visited lorry man to pick up colour cards for horsebox make-over. He didn't recognize me as I turned up in sports car this time – stereotype of person driving pink horsebox obviously doesn't fit with Honda S2000 convertible. Intended to go for cheapest paint option but couldn't stop myself from choosing beautiful metallic colours. Total inability to limit expenditure!

Also, went into town and bought some wonderful fabric to cover triptych screens being made for small cottage windows, in lieu of curtains. Fabric which drew my attention (red with embroidered gold balls on it) was called Suzanne, my late mother's name. So, I will take it as a sign – of what, I don't know! In fact, I went mad and ordered three different shades of Suzanne for three screens.

Later the same day, made it to my sunset seat (far corner of riding arena) to bathe in natural beauty. Magical view of the valley beyond (could be the Amazon Forest but it's the Welsh borders). Gentle warm breeze blowing. Looked around to see Benje and my two cats sitting behind me. Mused on D's description of my house as the 'magic castle'. Children said it was like something from *The Lion, The Witch & The Wardrobe*. It is, a bit.

7th June

A 5am start for London today. Long day. It's now 1.30am as I write, with another early start coming up as Sam has a day off, so I'm on horse duty. Will invoke perfect sleep in the time available – it usually works!

London was great. Not so many external meetings this time but individual catch-ups with everyone in the business, albeit brief, to see where all are at. Lengthy meeting with newest director. A joy to see her in full flow. Only been with the company 7 months but a real powerhouse. I recognized her potential when I interviewed her despite being quietly spoken and petite – not that size has anything to do with it. "Great things come in little packages", my mum used to say. She was 5'1" and her mother was even smaller. I inherited the 'small' gene which hasn't always been a blessing, especially in sport. But perhaps lack of stature, in my case, was compensated by a stronger will to win?!

The theory is that the new director is succession planning for me, a means of taking a back seat in the business and, in due course, selling it with a proven management team in situ. The director, who I will refer to as 'A', is doing a lot of what I would be doing if I was in the business full-time, combining overview stuff with the nitty-gritty. It's a great skill to develop, not only for those in management but for everyone in the business in their respective roles. 'A' has sat in on everything I have done, since she started. She knows the culture now and is starting to drive the organisation forward (in conjunction with the two other directors who have been working closely with me, since being promoted to board positions). During this time, we have made decisions collectively, which has been an excellent team-building exercise, not to mention essential, in order to pass on the reins of power.

Often, the person who starts an organization and builds it to a certain level is not always the best person to move it forwards. 'A's ideas are spot-on for where the company is now and the market we are in. She's more tuned in to the market than I, because my creative energy is now focused on reinventing myself in new areas (including broadcast and mentoring, which I have been itching to move into for the last 4 or 5 years). So, I have more of a facilitating role in the company now, which I really enjoy. It's fun to be supporting rather than driving.

I was meant to have lunch with a dear friend (businesswoman, homeopath, kindred spirit and glorious human being), to discuss the possibility of succeeding her as Chair of a prominent London-based women's network. I was really into networking in the early '80s – great for meeting potential clients, peer group inspiration and making contacts.

At that time, I founded and ran a network myself for women in financial services. Loved pushing myself out of my comfort zone and asking famous women to speak, chairing debates which were held in committee rooms of the House of Commons, getting a national award scheme off the ground and lots more. All activities were sponsored, so free to members. It grew like topsy and did a lot to raise the profile of women in financial services and identify the special style and skills they bring to their work and to leadership.

The friend in question didn't show, as she forgot to write it in her diary. So, as I had allocated the time, I dragged an admiring male friend out from a nearby office to have lunch with me instead. Wonderful to be adored, albeit briefly! Enjoyed being all-woman. Find it hard to remember early business years now, when I was more in 'androgynous' mode and, at times, used a lot of male energy. Could only access the woman part of me in infrequent lucid moments. Stems from growing up thinking 'feminine' was weak (the negative side of my parents' relationship) and, conversely, believing power belonged to men – neither of which is true.

During those formative years, I disliked seeing women use their sexuality to get on at work (the other end of the spectrum). Looking back, many didn't believe they had an option as it really was a man's world, especially in finance (and still is). Now, I definitely advocate owning your femininity (in the broadest sense) and using the power of it in business, as you then have access to intuition (a female attribute) which is far more fun and effective than using willpower, along with a host of other uniquely female attributes that are so needed in the world right now.

Funnily enough, I have learned a tremendous amount about feminine energy from my mare Nicky. She is the ultimate 'girl' and matriarch in horse terms. Animals are such good teachers. She does the full range, from kind, loving, generous and 'sweet as pie' (batting those long eyelashes of hers) to total m-a-r-e! She also uses her unabashed power to control the other horses in the field, so there is no disputing, not for a second, who is boss. All who meet her, people and horses alike, understand they are her minions and there to do her bidding. She is a very, very regal creature and expresses her power absolutely through her posture and gestures. I have watched and learned what to emulate and what to avoid.

Changing the subject, today was election day. Despite the fanfare, it's a non-event for me as no party is inspiring enough to vote for. Politics has lost the plot, along with much else in our world. However, I wanted to exercise my right to vote (won through blood, sweat and tears of my pioneering sisters), so I allowed my pendulum to decide where to cast a vote for best effect and highest good of humanity. Basically, my pendulum is my instinct on the end of a piece of string which has access to a far bigger picture than I do!

8th June

A tiring day doing the horses. Crawled into bed at 2am after catching up with work. 5 hours sleep again and up early to brief Laura (weekend groom). Physically tired but mentally alert.

Two lame horses today. Bummer! Ollie has sore feet after being re-shod. He has very thin soles. May just get sound in time for his dressage competition next Tuesday. Hoping enthusiasm on the day makes up for lack of preparation. Nicky is also lame – not sure why.

Did diagnosis with pendulum and came up with muscular strain in shoulder – probably got out of bed the wrong way, or a few too many somersaults in the field yesterday?

Did some energy healing on her and will see how she goes but must face dreadful possibility of not going to Longleat Horse Trials, long-awaited first event of the season after Foot and Mouth epidemic. Nothing else is near enough to get to for another month. Really missing adrenalin rush of cross-country jumping. Might be a blessing in disguise though, as pendulum also indicates emotional imbalance due to being in season, in which case, going to Longleat would break resolve of not competing a mare full of hormones. Horses! Boy, I wish they could speak.

Lots of work today, including an article for the company's quarterly magazine. One benefit of being boss is that I decide what I write about. Also, boring but important business rates appeal and never-ending emails (about 50). One email is from a co-director raising concerns about circulating each director's 6-month plan for their part of the business, to the whole company – full disclosure! Gave staff an overview at last company meeting of what senior managers do on a day-to-day basis (which is usually a mystery to them). Then thought, by circulating six-monthly plans, they will see we work every bit as hard as they do and also face challenges along the way. They can feed in ideas and feel more engaged in our collective progress, too. Good theory and worth trying. Must speak to doubting director, as other senior colleagues are on board.

Unannounced visit from *Local Lover (LL)* at lunchtime. Impeccable timing though no food passed our lips! Fab interlude – words fail me. Sun shining, off to town 'topless' (the car, not me) for weekly shop and some 'torture' thrown in for good measure – leg wax and bikini line. Men, you have no idea! Distract myself with nice thoughts and attempt to relax before each rip of the wax strip. However, muscles cave in and spasm just at the wrong moment so it really, really hurts and leaves horrid marks. Resemble a plucked turkey! Don't know why I bother as I never get round to wearing a bikini, or any swimwear at all. Vanity must be the answer, or maybe it's a little bit of loving myself as 'smooth feels good', or maybe to impress *LL*?

Arrived home to find horses have escaped from starvation paddock (they spend half the day there to keep their figures trim as grass is too rich at the moment). Got into field set aside for hay and completely pigged out. Also been in pond splashing each other and now filthy and in need of baths. Sorted and settled them for the night on reduced rations. They're not impressed and nor am I!

Had my supper in the garden watching the sun descend into the valley – spectacular. Then back to slaving over a hot computer. Almost forgot, I did a phone interview with *Woman's Hour* on Radio 4 about dramatic shift in work-life balance when I moved to the back of beyond. Crap signal in the house, so legged it to the car in the garage where signal a bit better and only just made it in time. First radio programme I've done which is not of a financial nature; symbolizes start of new career phase.

Email from psychic friend D who has tuned into my lame equines and come up with the following: It is resistance (manifesting as lameness) in both horses for different reasons. Ollie's is due to the tough decision I am making about him right now. I must tell him I love him and that I am only doing what I must do; also, that it is for the best for both of us. Nicky is resistant because if she takes time out to have a baby, she will be knocked off her perch as top performer on the yard, a dichotomy for her. Makes perfect sense, at least to me.

K-N-A-C-K-E-R-E-D. Bed and a lie-in, finally, I hope?!

11th June

8am. Caption would read 'Women at work'! Sam and I, equipped with hammer, nails and baler twine are fixing fence posts. Woman-power… we have the technology.

Message on answerphone from company solicitor to say he heard my interview on Radio 4 and was impressed about the company values bit. I didn't catch that part when I listened to broadcast version. Damn! Thought they had deleted it. They obviously cut back to me at the end of the programme after I switched off. Pleased it was included though.

L-o-v-e synchronicity, particularly lights on timers coming on as I walk into the room. To me they are symbolic of a greater universal force at work, the ultimate creative thingamajig. Another example of synchronicity today – while faxing arrangements to my gardener for the garden makeover next week, the phone rings and it's him. Telepathy works much faster than technology. In my utopian future, computers, faxes, mobile phones and the like would be obsolete. We would just use thought.

While on the subject of synchronicity, bumped into brother-in-law and nephews for the third time in two weeks, in town this afternoon. Am even more convinced that when you recognize small synchronistic events (often of no consequence) and know they are not just coincidences, you get more. It's a skill. You have to practise the art of expecting good things. Then you can apply the same to bigger ticket items like business, abundance and health, and manifest synchronicities of consequence to create them.

Have to be careful not to shoot ourselves in the foot though because when things matter, there's a tendency to be fearful about not having them. A strong desire for something is the pre-requisite for bringing it into your reality but angst about 'lack of' slows it down and can even cancel it. So simple, yet so profound. I know it works; I've experienced it many times. Even so, I don't always have the composure to make it happen. At least I'm more aware of why I'm getting what I'm getting in my life now. Perfect practice makes perfect, and I will get better. Awesome stuff and very powerful.

No eventing! Both horses are still unsound. Devastated temporarily until I think of the extra day I will have and what I can do with it. I feel some spending coming on. Oh dear! Will also do hands-on healing on horses to speed recovery. Did you know that animals communicate telepathically, which is how my clairvoyant friends are able to tune in to them? Cats, dogs, horses and probably many other animals aren't limited to a range of miaows, woofs and whinnies; they see and receive information telepathically, mostly through pictures. But don't take my word for it, try it yourself with your pet.

Cats and dogs often know the precise moment their owner will arrive home and are waiting for them, or start barking, or meowing etc. Most animal lovers have experienced this. I first became aware of the telepathy thing many years ago when I was out riding with a friend and we met two other riders stabled at the same yard, who were returning home. We stopped and chatted for a while before carrying on in opposite directions. My horse and my friend's horse got very excited and pranced around on the spot as if they were getting ready to gallop. Interestingly, the other riders had just told us they had been to a Common and had a blast. The horses had swapped notes.

Since then, I have used pictures to communicate with all my animals. When the horses are stressed before setting off in the horsebox to a competition, I say their name to get their attention, then send a mental picture of the type of activity they are going to do (as if I am looking through their eyes) and they take a deep sigh and settle down – instant transformation. I had a wonderful horse (the first in my adult life) who I was especially in tune with and when I lunged him (horse goes round you in circles on the end of a long rope) I never had to utter a single word. I used to give him all the commands (to walk, trot, canter, halt) through pictures. It was truly amazing.

My animals send me pictures too – of feed and water buckets, of course (essential creature comforts), which rugs they prefer to wear and much more. It's a whole new dimension. When D stayed, she could understand them communicating with each other too. We went out riding (D on Ollie, me on Nicky). Nicky was agitated and stroppy, flicking her head and neck at Ollie – she is a very fast walker and poor Ollie was having to jog to keep up. I thought she was just being bossy but D said she was cross with Ollie for cheating. Horse logic!

12th June

Today is my self-imposed, slightly late deadline for getting the proposal to Radio 4 for the series of dialogues with top businesswomen. I've been focusing on it for a week or so but not thinking about the detail, just imagining producing the document quickly and effectively when I sit down to write it. Thought about how great it would feel to finish it. It worked. Two hours from start to finish including researching some potential interviewees. Hope he likes it.

Finished the day watching an eventing video by one of the world's leading lights. He focused on basic principles in training all his horses – from youngsters to superstars. Yet again demonstrates that consistency and repetition of simple principles produces outstanding results. You can get so much from watching top performers if you get into their mindset and the feeling of what it must be like to ride like them. I think it has the power to raise your game, even though you haven't experienced what they have.

Sport is a mind game, every bit as much as it is physical. In my rowing days, though I was small I still managed to beat many women who were much bigger and stronger than me. Technical ability and fitness are essential (being the best you can for what you have). But the rest is a mental game you play with yourself. Psyching out the opposition is irrelevant; it's about psyching yourself. Of course, when racing those who have same approach and have size on their side, no chance! But I did much better than I should have, for my size.

15th June

Shopping. Forgot I hate the 'madding crowd' when shopping in cities. Went out with clear intention of buying a chair – a sitting, thinking and meditation chair for my healing room. I have been imagining this chair for some time and knew I would recognize it when I saw it. As I went down the escalator to the basement of the store, the chair leapt out and beckoned to me. A small brown leather armchair with a velvet cushion and very expensive looking. Not a chair I could have imagined but absolutely perfect – aesthetically pleasing, comfortable and the right size for my slight personage; a chair which would encourage me to sit down for periods in excess of five minutes and be still. One small mortgage later (and I am not entirely sure it will fit through the narrow cottage doors of my house), I am the proud owner of a 'life-long' thinking and meditation chair.

16th June

Expecting my sister and her clan to show up and bring their ex-army Landrover which will live with me while they are renting a house in town (it's also my escape route when it snows, as gorgeous minute sports car doesn't cope with the white stuff). Made a massive and particularly tricky poppy-seed cake for the occasion. They didn't show up. Disappointed but it's a family right to be unreliable. Poppy seed cake relegated to the freezer.

Hurray! Just passed 10,000 words of writing though paying the price in sleep deprivation. The whole process is amazing. I am loving it. Have been planning to write a book for years and done various proposals. One was even accepted by a publisher, but I didn't proceed as couldn't take my eyes off the 'business ball' at the time. Also, the thought of writing a treatise, even on a subject of interest, seemed very dull.

A few months ago, when staying with a girlfriend in London, I was persuaded to take the project off the backburner. "Now is a good time as it symbolizes new beginnings" she said. The next day, I put out for inspiration for a book idea that would be fun and painless. Instantly, the thought of an autobiographical diary came to mind. Daily life is very easy to write about and I feel inspired to talk about how I am dealing with things that are uber current. Sorry if I'm boring you?

Listened to a repeat of the Radio 4 interview this evening. Yes, they did cut back to me at end to include the bit about my business values. Interviewer implied it was OK for small businesses but not relevant for big business, and I disagreed. I said our principle of equal importance of staff, clients and profit applies to all sizes of business and is good for everyone *and* the bottom line.

Going outside now to play football with Benje, do horses and enjoy last of another gorgeous sunset. Benje limping after vicious tackle of the football. Quick blast of hands-on healing and in a few minutes he sprints off, perfectly sound. I'm gob-smacked. This stuff always surprises me. Flash back to a few years ago at a Horse Trials, when jumping cross country... my horse tripped on landing over a fence and cut his knee on a flint. In fact, he snagged an artery in his knee. Blood was flowing like a river. Very scary! I hadn't done much healing then, just the odd scratch or bang on myself but while waiting for the vet to come and amidst shouts of "Put a tourniquet on him" I clasped my hands around his knee and imagined the blood clotting, for all I was worth.

When I took my hands away minutes later, the bleeding had stopped and the blood had clotted – it felt like treacle. I leapt around whooping like a kid with a new toy, struggling to believe my eyes. The vet struggled to believe his too. He cleaned the wound and bandaged the leg and I continued with daily healings for a week. The knee quickly healed without stitches or infection.

That was my first major experience of healing using the power of thought. Another one several years later, was when I was injured and it also involved horses. My horse was saddled up in the trailer at a competition. I lowered the ramp to get him out and realised I had forgotten to put the restraining bar up in front of his chest (which I took down to give me more room to get his saddle on). He launched himself onto the ramp and I reached up to grab him. As he rushed out, he spun around because he was still tied up inside and the end of my finger, from below the last knuckle, rotated clean off. I remember looking at it and thinking, "Oh, f-word! That's not easily fixable".

I put the end back on the white bone (which, surprisingly, doesn't come right to the end of your finger) and led my horse over to some people I knew. I gave them the keys of my car and asked if they would take my horse and trailer home and if someone else would drive me to hospital. I managed to retain my composure on the 45-minute journey to A&E with lots deep breathing and focusing my attention on clotting the blood, de-sensitising the finger and keeping it infection-free.

I must have arrived at the hospital looking like something out of Jilly Cooper's novel *Riders* (wearing full competition kit – white breeches, jacket and hat). I had stopped the bleeding and the end of my finger was duly stitched back on. There was very little pain and it healed with fully functioning nail and nerves, much to everyone's amazement (including me), in just a few months. If you are thinking of trying this 'trick' at home, don't – a bruise or a cut will suffice to begin with. Just visualize the affected area being perfect. Your cells will do the rest!

17th June

Knocked out regular Q&A mentoring piece, first thing. Chose to do one on someone's difficult relationship with their parents. Been through enough of that myself so whizzed off the answer – well, one answer anyway. Certainly, a key issue for me was getting to know my parents as people. For most of my adult life, whenever I met them, I seemed to regress to age 17. Not surprising as this was when I last lived at home and, since then, I had withheld certain personal information about my life. So, their only frame of reference was 'me as a teenager'.

I found the best way to get to know them as adults was to spend time with each of them separately, so they didn't compete for attention and we didn't slip into old parent-child patterns; also, I could then have a completely open dialogue. If asked, I told everything – minus a *LL* or similar!

Off to lunch somewhere in the middle of nowhere with another 'off-the-wall' friend (artist, healer, psychic) and her father. Actually, met the dad first as he was my only neighbour at a previous home. He became a beloved surrogate father and one of my best friends despite the massive age gap. Retired last week in his late 70s as Chairman of a huge privately owned and (unusually) benevolent conglomerate – one of the few left from a bygone colonial era. Hopefully, he's going to write a book to capture some of his extraordinary life and times.

His daughter has become a friend and we have been pals through various periods of change, as we're on the same wavelength. My turn to support her this time through a major turning point in her life – a man, of course, is the catalyst!

Got home and straight onto a hot computer to deal with zillions of emails including one about the Q&A I wrote. Though they liked my answer, newspaper didn't feel it was businessy enough, even though original agreement had been for me to cover whole-people issues. Bummer! Under duress, I dream up another subject – 'The art of delegation' seems like a safe idea.

Visit from *Local Lover (LL)*. He arrived in pain. Had been injured and was suffering. Surprised he accepts my offer of hands-on healing. Must be seriously uncomfortable. Won't be up to usual tricks!

19th June

Ollie, Heather and I set sail at 8am in the pink (soon to be blue) horsebox en-route to a dressage competition. Glorious sunshine and hot too, which means hideous white skin (mine) exposed in shorts and vest. Onlookers will need sunglasses! Soul-searching discussion with Heather about crossroads in her career. Must decide where to channel her efforts. Is talented in dressage, eventing and showjumping, which is rare and a dilemma. Past disappointments still haunt her and are probably getting in the way.

Talked about lining energy up. Three elements to the process of creation, in my experience. First is to work up a strong passion for desired outcome by focusing on 'what' it will feel like and not 'how' it will happen. Second, stay balanced – somewhere close to happy but definitely not negative. If negative thoughts creep in, distract yourself back into balance by finding things that make you smile, or are calming. Appreciation works too. There is always something or someone to say 'Thank you' for, which is the 'glass half full' approach to life. When you are balanced, you are in touch with your instinct, and this leads to signposts. Basically, your instinct nudges you to do this or that, go hither or thither until you bump into coincidences that are not really coincidences at all. This is synchronicity which you have created, and recognising and acting on it is the third part of the process.

If we were masters in this art, we'd be able to manifest with ease what we want in our lives – at the appropriate time, of course. Thought is energy. It interacts with a field of infinite potentials created by everyone else's dreams, aspirations and thoughts and we magnetise things from this which match our focus. This is a 'divine helping hand', which will probably be explained by quantum physics one day. However, as mere mortals, we have doubts and fears that diminish our intent, so it can take a long time to manifest what we want, and sometimes never. I expect I'll be practising all my life, and many more to come.

Arrived home to find a hive of activity in the garden. A truck load of plants has just been delivered, and an army of people are digging borders; the patio team is grouting and a man on a ladder is painting window frames. Quite a sight. Garden under reconstruction after four years of waiting. I only have one thing to say... hurray!

20ᵗʰ June

Up early to get on the computer and go through content for a new internet site, part of my personal relaunching campaign. I've done a skills swap – technological wizardry in exchange for mentoring (obviously).

Man on ladder hard at work on windows. He's a TV actor really, who decorates in between jobs. Love it when people surprise you. Goes to show, you really can't make assumptions about anyone. But horrid smell in house from paint. Can feel stinging in my eyes and throat – had forgotten about organic, odourless alternatives. Suffered hell with allergies for 18 months during renovations when I first moved in. Either I have a vast capacity to let go of pain, or it's buried very, very deep and I have forgotten what it felt like? Damn!

Someone planting out the garden too. It's really taking shape. Scrappy bit previously in front of the magic view is now a fabulous rockery with beautiful stones found in my fields, and woodland plants, which have turned a nondescript patch into an oasis of tranquillity. Meanwhile, an old plough (type pulled by horses in days of yore) found in a shed, has been painted lilac by yours truly and is the centrepiece of new shrubbery. Lovely!

Call from neighbour. Benjamin is trying to have his way with a sheepdog bitch on heat nearby, who is meant to be working. Apparently, causing bedlam for the farmer (named Giles, yes, life is stranger than fiction) but great amusement for spectators, as sheep scatter in a multitude of directions. Not the idea. Go and retrieve a 'hot-dog' who is tired but happy.

Then off to the vet with Benje for some dog business. Receptionist laughed when I said he'd been scooting and I wanted his adrenal glands drained. Handsome young vet put me right, "They are anal glands *not* adrenals". Cringe with embarrassment. Benje not keen on 'anal sex' with vet's finger and funny how they always get the owner to hold the sharp end? Luckily, I left the surgery with all my fingers. Had to laugh when I discovered Benje's computer records refer to him as Benje Price! Does he look like his 'mother'?

After D's recent communications with Ollie, Sam (equine manager) has been trying her hand at some horse-talk herself. She's very good and came up with useful information. Hope she doesn't leave me to become a 'horse whisperer'! Apparently, Ollie would prefer one-to-one handling (currently has three of us riding and handling him – Sam, me and Heather) as he needs to form a strong bond with one rider/carer. This is why he's bonded so heavily to my mare Nicky, which is not ideal because she only wants him around when she's hormonal – tart! Needs calm handling, positive strong riding and a sense of security. Lack of security is reflected in his work. Because he isn't secure in himself, he can't always be brilliant, even though has the ability. Needs to feel special, though not necessarily put on a pedestal. Bit of an unsure character with a slightly dominant streak (can vouch for that when he recently did a rodeo act and bucked me off). But very sensitive, intelligent and kind, and needs to settle, which will take around a year. Wow! Kudos Sam. Makes perfect sense and gives me clarity on the type of buyer to look for.

Finally, while still on things equine, got an email from France with information about the stallion I want to use for Nicky's baby. He is a stunner and one of the top showjumping stallions in the world. Hairs on my back stand up whilst reading blurb and looking at his pictures. Lucky girl, though she'll miss the best bit, as it's frozen semen. Copied email to D who 'tuned in' and said "He's fabulous beyond compare – only sad thing is they cannot actually do it in the flesh; he yearns for a gal as much as she needs to be serviced." Funny! Perhaps she could be fulfilled next time with a stallion closer to home? Poor girl, not much difference between mares and women then?!

21st June

Two horses are sedated for serious dental work. Horrid to see them with heads on the floor and knees buckling plus a gag on, to open their mouths. But no choice. Big boy Harry is missing some teeth, as was kicked by another horse before I got him. So, has uneven growth (yes, horses' teeth grow). As Harry is not keen on having a rasp in his mouth and is strong enough to lift two people off the ground whilst trying, sedation is the only option. Ollie has sharp teeth at the back of his mouth which have bruised his gums. So, a lot of work is needed which would test his patience. Better to be safe than sorry. Will do some healing to neutralize effect of drugs and help both get over the trauma and discomfort. Poor boys!

Now that garden is two-thirds planted, dreaded watering vigil starts. After having ailing water pressure fixed, there is a downpour of rain – cosmic joke! Oops, spoke too soon, it's stopped so will have to use the hose, after all. And now water pressure has dropped again (as blood pressure rises) – what a laborious job. It takes forever.

Tomorrow it's London – unusual to do a Friday but tube strike changed plans and, annoyingly, the strike is now cancelled. Exasperation! How are you meant to do any business in London? Benje has done a bunk and I want to go to bed. Will have to go looking with a torch. Little monkey!

22nd June

Major cash flow crisis in the business. Figures are worse than expected; must get to bottom of it with other directors, particularly as just refinanced with the bank. Serious egg on face, pending. Defining moment.

Been working on calming myself since late last night when figures were faxed through and was overcome by panic. Must remember, been here before and it all turned out well. Focus on positive outcome. Work on eliminating negative thoughts and stopping myself dwelling on perils of delegating to management team when I carry the financial risk (contradiction in terms, but the price I paid for partial freedom).

Starting to feel better and thinking about good things that have been happening in the business and where we are going as a company. We are well constructed and managed, so this glitch will be sorted. One of those moments in life when you look over the edge of the cliff and decide you don't want to go there. Momentarily thinking of the wonderful home I have just finished and the thought of losing it; losing hard-earned lifestyle and having to start all over again. D-E-F-I-N-I-T-E-L-Y NOT!

In London, first meeting of the day is with an angel – a man who has come to fix my computer. Don't know how people do such a frustrating job, must be a 'techno-man' thing. Then, moment of truth and dreaded directors' meeting. Decided to build up to the main issue by dealing with minor housekeeping items first and anything that can be solved quickly to get us into 'solutions orientated' mode. This means figures after lunch – better not eat much!

Lunch with friend who didn't show last week. We discuss me taking over from her as Chair of national women's network. Said she would stay on as Vice Chair (great plan as I love her dearly and have worked with her before in another network). Brainstormed her management dream team but radical measures required to get the network back on track. Seems to be the theme 'du jour'! Shame, as it's one of the best professional women's networks around. Would be good to carry on her work and revitalize things. On a different note, she's off to a tantric sex workshop this weekend (fun or what?!). Best of all, she's going to introduce me to a very eligible man she knows who works in diamonds and is in touch with his spiritual side – now there's an unlikely combination. But 'a girl's best friend' and all that.

'Crunch time'! Tell myself to be light and breezy to set tone for second part of directors' meeting. Invoke divine intervention to bring clarity and a positive outcome. Nuts of it is down to under performance at the end of the tax year, which is a hitherto unheard-of experience for us, as this is normally the busiest time of the year. But same experience suffered by many in the sector this year due to poor stock market and legislative changes. However, a rather large error in management accounts was also discovered, a result of mistaken communication between directors. Re the former, we will develop new business strategies to prevent any future reliance on seasonality. Re the latter, we'll have to put it down to 'team learning' and recover.

In the past, I did the figures as didn't have co-directors until recently. This year we did them together and, between us, missed something each thought the other had taken care of. Gutted is an understatement but delegation means giving people permission to make mistakes. This is a biggie and will be costly. Still, it's not about blame. Just need to deal with it.

End meeting by declaring complete faith in management team and the business and ask all to confirm their support, or otherwise! All are right there. Must take eyes away from 'cliff edge' now and focus on solutions. Check how I feel in the pit of my stomach (best indication of how things really are) – feels fine and clear. Have learned to trust this. Will have to increase guarantees with bank and possibly lend company some money from proceeds of shares recently sold to co-directors. Not life-threatening, so not the end of the world, I guess?

Exhausted and sleep on the train on way home. Amazes me how the most private of events, ie sleeping, is done so publicly by so many (including me). Dread waking up with a snort, which I have done on past occasions and tried to disguise as a sneeze. A quick hello (or rather goodnight) to dozing horses and onto the computer while bath water goes cold. Heck, is that the time?

23rd June

Entirely physical day, so knackered body to match knackered mind now. No help with horses, hence an early start which wasn't ideal after hitting the sack at 2am. Also, had to crack on before garden team arrived for penultimate assault. Later, chained to a hot stove to cook lunch for an impromptu visit from father, his girlfriend and her teenage daughter. Scraped out remaining contents of fridge and turned out tuna tart with wild rice, broccoli and a salad, plus a smelly cheese platter, fruit salad and poppy seed cake from freezer (for those with no conscience). No one managed the cake, so Sam and I will make a sizeable hole in it tomorrow. Pity my father who is trying to watch his waistline, as next stop is my sister's – for tea!

Love seeing my father (in small doses) and delighted he's so happy with his new lady. He's a young 71-year-old who's just completed an MBA, for fun – it's anything but, I know, I did one. Girlfriend is considerably younger and moves in next month. They are very compatible, so say all of us (me, my sis' and bro'). Mum died 5 years ago of leukaemia. Father had one relationship afterwards which didn't work out but he got clear about what he didn't want, which led him to find what he did. Result! Has gone through a lot of personal growth (ironically, he's now more the person he would have liked to have been with Mum) and is much happier. Very pleased for him.

They leave and I dash to the yard to get Ollie in from the field for exercise. I am given the merry run-around in the field as his idea of bliss on a sunny afternoon doesn't coincide with mine. Eventually outwit him and he's cornered. Went for a good long hack to build up fitness. Ollie's not done much riding out, so can be a bit hairy at times. I visualise returning home safely.

Get back to find garden crew tidying up. It's a dream come true, or at least it will be in 2 to 5 years' time when everything has grown (well, whatever survives, that is). Spent a fortune on plants as it's a massive garden but prefer to do things in complete projects, rather than in stages. Suits my nature which is basically impatient and also tidy (OK, perfectionist). Later, it takes nearly two hours to water it all. Not so thrilling!

Benje's nagging me to go out as it's time to do late night horse shift and tuck the girls and boys up. He's playing cute – eyes are moving from side to side with eyebrows rising and falling simultaneously. Expression reads, "Will you please hurry up! I spend my life waiting for you." Soooooooon, Benje, soon.

I would be lying if I said business problems hadn't drifted in and out of my mind today. Working hard to stay balanced. Conscious of checking how I feel in the pit of my stomach at regular intervals and noticing when there is tension. Search for positive things to focus on to improve the mood. Know that if I lose balance, I will disconnect from my instinct which I need to guide me to the solution. Did, however, do a brief meditation on the business first thing this morning and came up with an idea which might be the start of a plan. Will focus on it a bit more and see if it has legs.

Phone call from girlfriend who shares my slightly wayward outlook on life. Her sister has been told she has cancer. Spend time talking about ways of supporting the sister. I read about someone recently who was terminally ill and was given six months to live. He asked for all the comedy videos that could be found and watched the lot – laughed continuously. Four months later, his symptoms had vanished. Laughed himself back to health. Seriously!

A true story of 'spontaneous remission'. He let go of the fear of dying (fear inhibits healing) and created as much joy as he could which also distracted him. Under these conditions, his body regained its balance which, by definition, is a healthy state where there can be no illness. I believe that most illness comes from long-term emotional imbalance, or imbalance from external factors such as toxins in the environment, food or water. This impairs the immune system and, as I understand it, creates changes in the blood which impact on the genetically weakest system or organ in the body, manifesting illness. There is a broader spiritual perspective too – a discussion for another time!

24th June

Failed abysmally to avoid feeling gloomy today. Had a few lucid moments when I was distracted by things such as fabulous sunny day, horses very sweet and doing their best to amuse me, Nicky sound after two weeks (and in season again, I don't believe it!), sister and her troop calling in for tea (really scraped the barrel this time, leftovers from lunch yesterday, including remaining crumbs of poppy seed cake), brilliant sunset, garden radiant after another mega watering, ritual candlelit bath with lavender and a meditation. But in between all that, I felt a large threatening cloud over my head.

Tomorrow is another day and a chance to bounce back – one day of dampened spirits is the max I can afford. There is too much at stake. At least it is occasional days now, whereas malaise might have lasted weeks in times gone by. I know that only I can dig me out of a hole. Today was definitely a low point. Try to focus on a 'happy ending' – remember past examples of getting out of difficult scrapes. Banish fleeting thoughts of losing house, and a life without horses. Ask for divine inspiration. Must regain balance. Wrote on a sticker next to my computer, "I trust self to know how and when to act". Fall asleep over keyboard...

25th June

Saw *Local Lover (LL)* first on official business (yes, we do have official business), then well... you guessed. Failed to cheer me up. However, at 11am, I suddenly felt bright, focused and back on track. Weird! Later, when I spoke to D she also had a low weekend and felt better today, curiously at about the same time. Decided there must have been some retrograde astrological influences which cleared, that had exacerbated things?

Though up and down a bit during the day, generally much improved – balance almost restored. Inspired enough to write sponsorship proposal for another women's network I'm launching in September. Women are still few and far between in the financial sector. The world of money is perceived as hostile and male. Financial men have a reputation for being patronizing (amongst other things); also, many women suffer from 'maths phobia', as I did originally. I had a poor maths teacher at O level which caused me to lose confidence with all things numerical. Probably some social conditioning too, that maths isn't a girl's subject. Thereafter, I struggled with statistics as part of a psychology degree and emerged from business school with an MBA thinking I was the only graduate who couldn't read a balance sheet. Glad to say, having landed in the financial world, I have overcome this issue!

No figures update today. I'm told they will come in the next couple of days. Meantime, discussions about underlying assumptions fly back and forth. Directors faced another challenge today after discussion with a staff member about changing her role. She isn't keen. They acted with best intentions but she wants to leave. Blast! Will do my best to find a way through as she is a valued team member. Might ask her to be the administrator for new network when it's up and running, which would really suit her. There is also another role we'll need in next 6 months, so could bring this forward on a trial basis, as an option. Hate situations like this but can't please everyone all the time. Proud of directors though, they worked well together.

On the horse front, arranged for equine physiotherapist to see Ollie tomorrow to get to the bottom of an issue that's been niggling for a while. Also, took Lady Penelope to the garage for her makeover. Will look fab in metallic midnight blue with mint green stripes and silver wheels. No more comments about pink and yellow trim looking like an ice-cream van! Will also blend into the landscape better when parked at home. Rode Nicky after two weeks off. Was a right madam but we kissed and made up after.

More girl-power! Yours truly perilously poised with one foot on top of ladder in guest bedroom, armed with hammer and nails to fix a drape between two beams over bed. Other foot on wobbly headboard. Aiming to create four-poster effect. I like it.

Been feeling cold all day despite the sun. Think it must be effect of the business shock working its way from emotional to physical. Man still up ladder outside painting windows, while I do yet another watering vigil. Oh, let there be rain – please!

26th June

Physio found nothing wrong with Ollie, so plot thickens. Social visit in the evening from *Local Lover (LL)* which successfully reached parts other things don't, this time. Big smile!

27th June

First day of two-day residential training course in Georgian mansion in the most exquisite riverside location. Hate courses and conferences and can safely say have only been on two or three in twenty years of business and this is the first residential one. They always remind me how boring university was (not helped by going twice, BA then MBA – both huge disappointments).

This is a 'women leaders' course and staggeringly expensive, I have to say. But as I am starting a new career, part of which is mentoring executive and business women, it seemed a good idea to plug into current thinking and make new contacts amongst senior HR managers who are likely to attend. Strangely enough, I'm enjoying it and meeting some interesting people. Start to feel energized, very energized, in fact. Just the tonic after recent business crisis.

Also, bit of a mini-break as haven't been on holiday for years – lost count of how many. Living in the countryside seems to make holidays unnecessary on the one hand, but difficult to go away when you have animals, on the other.

Some findings and musings from the day, in no particular order:

- Discovered that state-of-the-art business thinking has caught up with my business thinking – or maybe it's just a woman's perspective? My company seems to tick all the boxes on the 'Transformational Management' checklist eg charisma, openness, inclusion, vision, people development, client care etc. Must send email to directors to tell them. They will be chuffed. Seems we are a cutting-edge culture. Just need to nail the profit thing.
- Top leaders display high scores on something called emotional intelligence (new term). They are personable, considerate, inclusive, charismatic and use a high degree of intuitive decision-making. I like to think I demonstrate those attributes! Maybe I need to ask colleagues? Difficult to teach intuition because the way we all receive it is different (though it's more natural for women) but I believe it can be facilitated, which is a strong theme in my version of mentoring.
- All this connects to my Radio 4 proposal which is essentially about finding 'secret ingredient X' through dialogues with top businesswomen. This research will be useful.
- Seem to have a fan club which is a happy discovery. A few people I know raved about my business when they introduced

me to other delegates. I cringed (noticeably) and wanted the floor to swallow me up, feeling unworthy given our current financial situation. Lots of positive influences all around though, so crawled out of hole quicker than normal and feel good again now. A lesson in how easy it is to do this, especially when surrounded by like-minded positive people. We over-complicate life.

- Focused on making contacts at this event. Created intention before I came, to link up with potential clients for the business and my personal mentoring. Have gained four potential financial clients and eight possible mentoring clients so far, as well as speaking to a senior corporate woman about a non-executive directorship position.

- Gorgeous looking man (one of only two guys on the course) who looks beautifully formed in all departments (using my X-ray vision). Definite sexual tension between us despite sitting on different tables (glances etc.) Adds interest! All breaks so far spent networking, so will have to find another way of talking to him.

- Getting into abundance mentality again. Realising there are infinite ways of doing fun, meaningful work and earning a good income. Remind myself money is not an issue. Money, fun, fulfilment, happiness and love are all possible. Nothing has to be sacrificed for something else. It's all in the mind.

- Most speakers use visual aids which is tedious and something I vowed I would never do, after falling asleep in countless university lectures through 'slide overdose'. Boring, boring, boring! A spontaneous speaker is infinitely preferable. You learn much more if you can tune into the energy of the person through their openness and passion for their subject. It's difficult to connect with an automaton who reads off slides. Only one, so far, has spoken with real passion and the audience was spellbound for over an hour.

Just overheard two women talking in the loos. One said she is on secondment to a major retailer which has "real vision and buzz". She thought they were all on pills! The other couldn't imagine what it would be like to work for a business that has passion and what that could achieve. Clearly, this is rare. What a sad state of affairs. Surprises me, as I have never been an employee.

At dinner, I find myself sitting opposite the gorgeous man. Despite a slightly squeaky voice which was a bit of a shock (didn't imagine it would come from *that* body), got on brilliantly and eventually acclimatized to his voice. Definitely on same vibe, every which way. Bit of a cheeky edge to the conversation!

Back in my room, finally got company's new financial forecast. Been waiting (painfully) for days. One of the directors just phoned. Looks pretty yuck for a while but better to know than to guess. We can now focus on turning things around. It's my job to deal with the bank, of course, so I will need a major session with directors to prepare. All of us feel a sense of relief knowing the true situation. The past is history, what matters is what we do now. Will sleep better tonight.

28th June

Arrived in the seminar room to find seating arrangements had changed. Sign said, 'Pick another table and expand your network'. A few seconds later *the* man sat down next to me. Heart skipped a beat. If the session gets boring, I can always fantasise... might do that anyway!

A non-academic day and some excellent businesswomen speakers. Two women had built businesses in excess of £20M turnover from scratch, with no previous business experience. Survived and thrived on their wits. Like me, discovered you make it up as you go. My business (heading towards £1.5 million) pales into insignificance in size. But it's a relative concept. Remind myself that in business and life, whatever the circumstances, we're all dealing with 'stuff'. How you manage yourself, people and situations is key. Everything else is a variation on this theme, including the size of your business. By and large, I think that what we get in life matches our capacity to deal with it (even if we don't know that at the time). So, comparing ourselves to others is meaningless. We (and our situations) are all different.

To family and friends, I seem to have a lot going on but I think this is because I have a large appetite for change. Even when it's painful, I know I am learning, and I always want to know more about myself and the world I live in. This is a big driver for me. Others seem to have uneventful lives but their lives probably provide plenty of challenge for them. I like this view. It avoids judgement and keeps a sense of humility.

Got on well with gorgeous man throughout the day and swapped email addresses. Left early – had enough of the whole conference thing by mid-afternoon. Drove home 'topless' in the sunshine, enjoying secret fantasies.

Called into bustling local market town on the way back to stock up on provisions. Small and local means the newsagent knows I buy slim fax paper rolls and the checkout staff at the supermarket know I like to pack my own shopping. You can't beat community.

Got home feeling great and rushed around to see which new plants had flowered, also to say hello to Benje, horses and cats. Then straight onto computer to follow up new contacts made and check emails. One from Radio 4. Opened it with bated breath. It said they really like the proposal and just one more hoop to go through. WOW!

Email gorgeous man and invite him to visit me and the furry entourage but because I don't know his personal circumstances, give him an opt-out by saying "If the invitation is inappropriate, I understand". Try to appear casual.

29th June

Sister phones. Conversation is about middle child (5-year-old) who seems depressed. Doesn't help he's just seen his head teacher have a heart attack in the school assembly and no explanation given to the children. Sister uses Angel cards, like me. These have words on them like strength, courage, flexibility, fun. Idea is to put them face down and pick one that attracts you, to help solve a problem intuitively. The word you pick indicates what to do or the energy to use. Though only five, my nephew understands the concept and has picked 'Power' three times in a week. Neither of them has sussed out the meaning yet. He finds everything easy and is liked by classmates. I feel he needs a way to channel his energy and feel his power, which is missing at the moment.

When you feel your power, it's awesome and inspiring. Depression is about resistance to something and it blocks you, so your life doesn't flow. He went to gymnastics for the first time last week and was talent-spotted. So, he's going to pursue this and I'm sure it will restore his mojo.

Headed out to the stables to speak to Sam about what horses are doing today. We have words. Apparently, I was abrupt last week. But I feel it's a misinterpretation. Perhaps business pressures precipitated a different tone than normal? On Sam's side, she has recently split with her man, so could be a bit sensitive. Had a good talk and I promptly burst into tears. How embarrassing but tears obviously an outlet for other issues too. It's 'one all', as Sam cried on me when she left her man. Feel much better now though. Sam is only 24 but I consider her a friend. She is wise and a kindred spirit. I think we somehow attracted each other into our lives. Sometimes parallel stuff going on and we provide a mirror for each other and support.

Phone call from psychic friend D. Amongst other things, told her about physio's findings, or lack of, for Ollie. She tuned into him and said his jumping problem (ie ambidextrous knocking down of show jumps) is to do with the way he is built. One of those things you just have to live with and accommodate. Won't solve it with treatment.

Not cut out for showjumping, period! Copes with the cross country jumping and hunting because it's more exciting, blood is up and jumping from speed from a slightly shallower angle, so easier for him. More useful information to help me find new home for him which plays to his strengths.

Blaring music coming from somewhere outside, even though I'm in the middle of the sticks. On investigation, farmer Giles is the culprit. He's checking sheep and has left music on full blast in his truck. Try not to focus on it or let it affect my peaceful mood. Off to do horses which is a convenient distraction.

1st July

Uncharacteristically, I am tired. Walking round in a daze and managed to smash two favourite pieces of crockery, something I *never* do. Clearly, need rest but soonest can do is next weekend. Got mentoring Q&A to write by 9am tomorrow, before Heather comes to train Ollie. We are also taking photos of him to place an advert in the press. Then need to go through company accounts to trim expenditure and check assumptions yet again, in preparation for directors' meeting on Tuesday. Been dreading doing this all weekend. Hoped to have done it already but as I was on horse duty (Sam's day off) and had to work out colour scheme for office which is being painted tomorrow (settled on bright yellow, pink, orange and terracotta to my own design for maximum creative energy), haven't got round to it yet. Also, have to prepare a mailshot for new women's network. Why is every day so short?

Rode Ollie today as well – was a complete prat! Went out hacking and he's taken to showing his displeasure at things by standing on his hind legs. No joke on a horse his size. Then he decided that going sideways was even more fun and we ended up in the middle of the hedge. Wouldn't go forwards at all, so made him reverse a long way down the lane until he got tired and gave in. He's at equivalent age of terrible teens and pushing boundaries, using any excuse to 'test mother' when riding out on his own, though never when doing favourite activity which is dressage. Had enough of that, so will put him on flower essences tomorrow to improve his mood They help to change the body's subtle energy fields including emotions.

I am naturopathic as far as possible – for me and my animals, and have had a lot of success using flower essences. I am also a big fan of homeopathy which works by giving instructions to cellular structure of the body (the 'smart body' that knows how to heal itself). At least, that's how I understand it. Suffice to say, both therapies work well for me and my furry family.

Must be a weekend for naughty horses. Yesterday, I couldn't catch Nicky. She galloped off at full pelt, bucking and squirting (horse expression for farting at speed) and set the other two horses off. Galloped until she was knackered. Does this quite a lot. Message is, "You'll catch me when I'm ready". Vivid recollection of an occasion in the past where, having failed to catch her during the day, I was getting desperate as night fell and the weather deteriorated. So, came up with radical plan to move her round the field with the quad bike to tire her out, hoping she would surrender. She didn't. Later on, phone call from neighbour saying he'd seen a light zooming around field and to be careful of hooligans. That's right – me!

Quiet moment in meditation room contemplating the future. Then, phone call from friend Sue who is down from London for the weekend at her nearby cottage. We'll meet for dinner tomorrow night with another girlfriend. Both are healers and psychics. Should be fun.

Gagging for bed...

2nd July

Pig of a day! Completely lost my composure and in a panic all day (even put knickers on inside out). Felt like a swarm of wasps were buzzing round my head, closing in on me. Should know better but a reminder to 'learn what you teach, practise what you preach' – my mantra!

Got Q&A done by 9.15am, only quarter of an hour behind target. This time, questions on improving performance and dealing with a colleague with body odour! Then did two telephone interviews. One with *Red* magazine. Hand signals from Sam halfway through phone call to say she'd got tractor bogged at the end of the field. Thankfully, decorator went to the rescue.

Second interview done on mobile phone while watering the garden. Also, had a call from a business school randomly asking if I was interested in being a director of their MBA programme. Where did that come from? Anyway, makes me laugh and is flattering but "No thanks". Would have been interested in some involvement but not full-time. Also, potential conflict of interest as I am on Board of Trustees for the business school where I did my MBA. Nice to be asked though. Dead bird on floor in kitchen, feathers everywhere courtesy of feline huntress. Yet again, "A woman's work is never done".

Heather rode Ollie with the aim of getting some good photos. Both looked very smart. Ollie sported a plaited mane which Sam did in fifteen minutes, breaking the world high-speed plaiting record. But he's a little out of practice with his work and it proved difficult to get the perfect shot for the advert. Will have to go back to two sessions of dressage training per week until he's sold, to ensure he's on form when people come to try him. Saddler arrives to do repairs on various bits of horse tack, and I dismantle and vacate my office for painting, which is disorientating.

People arrive to buy some of last year's hay crop, as I need room for this year's in the barn. Record harvest last year (1650 bales) from 15 acres due to amazing weather. Consequently, had to beg overflow storage from various neighbours as my barn only holds 600. Rode late afternoon in search of a brief quiet moment. Still haven't done company figure-work for meeting with directors tomorrow, will have to do it on train to London so, this time, definitely need to stay awake. Looking forward to evening out with friends tonight.

Just back, had a lovely time. Two women healers who are also conventional professionals. On way home, figured out a couple of contributory factors to feeling off balance recently (apart from financial crisis). First, I'm allergic to decorating stuff and there's nasty exterior paint on outside windows at the moment which, of course, smells in the house. Have had streaming nose and itchy eyes on and off which I thought was hay fever, though I don't generally get this. B-I-G mental note to use organic paints in future.

Second thing is, my home is my sanctuary and as long as there is peace and order, I can deal with the chaos around me in business and life. But decorating brings chaos and mess to my inner sanctum and it feels like violation, even though it's obviously for a greater good.

Just been out to say goodnight to horses and feel calm and balanced now. Balmy evening. Midges out so must be getting warmer. Lit citronella sticks in the yard to keep midges away from horses. Otherwise, they have a 'feeding frenzy' and drive the horses crazy.

3rd July

Managed to stay awake and confront dreaded figures on the train to London, despite only 5 hours' sleep. Management meeting is first meeting of the day to agree reductions in expenditure and finalise short, medium and long-term plans for increasing business. Excellent meeting, did what we had to do in two hours.

Co-directors showing great stoicism, pragmatism and a committed, positive attitude. Marvellous! Delivering plan is, of course, another matter. All agree the experience, painful as it has been, is a springboard for new beginnings; we are now absolutely clear who has responsibility for what figures and ensuring they are done in a way which is easy to understand and check. Bottom line looks better. Need to speak to bank again soon but will wait and see how business production looks in next few weeks before arranging a meeting.

Next up, meeting with auditors to look at draft accounts. Not brilliant, obviously. But we are using a new accountant who has come up with some really good ideas on how to make a presentation to the bank. This person loves his job. What a blessing! To him, figures are just a way of understanding a business and its people. This is the first accountant in all my years in business who asked for a meeting to discuss the accounts and gave useful input. Funnily enough, had been looking for someone to do this sort of thing periodically and he just turned up. Love synchronicity. His firm could have sent anyone but they chose him.

Went to businesswomen's forum at lunchtime, run by a major newspaper. Great fun and fab guest speaker. Made good contacts for business and mentoring. Came away feeling uplifted. Another management meeting afterwards (in between trying to see all staff personally to check expected business production). This time, discussed day to day things, eg training, staff issues, administration.

Later, supper with company's solicitor. Agreed to get staff from both our firms together to refer business each way. Then off to stay with D and her family who live in London. We talked forever and I finally went to bed with the dawn chorus. Back to work on three and a half hours sleep (I think it's a record). Coping well with sleep deprivation.

Previously, when extremely tired, used to get massive yawns where jaw nearly locked open. Gone past that now and appreciating time gained from sleeping less, generally. More sleep would be ideal but, in the circumstances, surviving on very little is a state of mind. Trick is instructing body to have all the rest needed in the time available, rather than saying must have 'x' number of hours to sleep. D is going to introduce me to a lovely man. Second friend who has promised this. Hope it's not the same one they both have in mind? Gorgeous person from the course didn't respond to email I sent, so assume I either scared him off or he is accounted for. Shame!

D's channelling is coming on really well now and we are having great fun tuning into all sorts of information – about horses, work, life and times. Channelling is the art of connecting with 'spirit' to bring through information from a broader perspective, in terms of wisdom and understanding; it's like asking an oracle. Sometimes the source is identified, sometimes it isn't. I facilitate by asking questions and supporting D as she's not always fully conscious of what is going on. So much incredible stuff has been channelled throughout history by human beings – in the Bible, of course but also in music, art and literature where the mastery surpasses mortal means. That's my explanation anyway.

I don't channel like D but I am aware that when I write or give talks, I often have thoughts I haven't had before, or say things I haven't said before, and wonder where they came from. Also, with mentoring, I often find myself giving 'inspired' advice, ie zoning in with pinpoint accuracy to core issues and fixes. A form of channelling, I would think and I am probably not alone in this experience?

4th July

On the man front, I bumped into a lovely one on the way to work. Coincidence? I don't think so. We used to talk to each other on the train when I commuted from another part of the country. Today, I went to get habitual cappuccino and croissant en route to the office but found the shop closed for refurbishment and had to go elsewhere. Lo and behold, there he was. The mind boggles to think how the universe lined that one up. We agreed to meet.

At the office, taught a colleague who has food allergies how to use a pendulum to dowse the foods that agree with her. It's a great tool. Piece of plastic (or crystal) on the end of a piece of string. Dowsing converts your instinct (internal guidance mechanism) into a form you can see. Colleague took to it like duck to water and was ecstatic. She had been to a Chinese herbalist who gave her a very strict diet to follow. Now, at least, she can dowse the degree to which each morsel of food is detrimental or beneficial and tailor her diet more precisely. She is going on holiday soon, so will use the pendulum to test food and avoid gippy tummy. We do more than personal finance in my company!

Big meeting in the afternoon with client-facing staff, who are all women. There are various means of raising issues and a few have emerged recently. So, this was the response slot. Generally went well, although one or two tricky moments including dealing with the cash-flow concerns they had become aware of. It's a fine line between giving too much and too little information. Staff need to know enough so they are comfortable but not too much that they panic. I explained it would take longer than anticipated to repay debt from moving premises and gave reasons. I also pointed out it's management's job to be concerned with the finances. They can help by remaining focused on business production. In bald terms, though I didn't say it, my house is on the line, not theirs and their jobs are not at risk. I explained we have been through this type of experience before a number of times, unbeknown to them and it's part of the growth cycle of most successful businesses.

5th July

A wonderful sunny day. The office at home is almost finished but orange will have to be toned down so less in-your-face, by adding a few embellishments. So, I'm going to paint a yellow design around the window which already has some pink on it. This is next to the orange wall, lemon window recess and green woodwork. Quite a heady mix. Definitely won't lack creative energy for working. Have decided to paint a yellow wave against terracotta on adjacent wall too. The whole thing will look great. Hard to describe.

Garden contractors are back today, and we discussed an unclaimed plot of land on the other side of the lane, opposite the house. I have decided to fence and clear the land (about an acre with a dilapidated cottage on it). I will improve it and claim title after 12 years, as permitted by law. Tried to find out who owns it. Various theories but no one knows and no records at Land Registry. Quite excited. Not only will it be prettier to look at when it's tidy and planted (it's a jungle at the moment) but, eventually, I could create a groom's cottage in place of the ruin. I am the only house it affects as it is 10 yards from my kitchen window. Beyond it, is a field.

Office is *still* not finished. Feeling dislocated without a proper workspace and resistant to working. The space around you is so important for productivity. Currently, using the phone socket in the hall with my computer propped on the windowsill to send emails. Not ideal.

Heather rode Ollie for another picture session today. He went really well this time, and I got some great shots for the advert. His work is coming on and he is much more focused. Hurray! Extra training has given him more presence and charisma. Really looks like a classy dressage prospect now.

A male friend is coming to take me out to dinner and stay over. Old flame from dim and distant past who has been a great chum ever since – one of the brightest and most caring people I know and now making loads of well-deserved money.

Can hear a dog snoring under a blanket at my feet. Must be bedtime, for both of us.

6th July

Had lovely meal in favourite bohemian eatery. Got back to find Aga had gone out. Damn! Could tell immediately I walked into kitchen, as it was stone cold. Thought I had run out of fuel but hadn't. Very pleased with myself, as I managed to get it going again but it probably needs servicing. Another item to add to the list.

I love my Aga. It's the first one I've had and I'm hooked. A beautiful piece of furniture which creates a toasty warm kitchen all year round, constant comfort for Benje and the cats and is always ready to cook on. Once you work out how (and don't incinerate everything) the food tastes so much better. And, no cooking smells. Aga cakes, for which I am renowned, are especially good and very moist. No end of other uses too, eg as a sauna if you open top oven and sit on a chair. Great for drying hair above the hot plate and, obviously, fab for drying clothes. Can't come to grief either as no flames, which is just as well. Last week, got back from London to find a note from Sam saying she couldn't find the meat I cooked for Benje's supper. That's because it was where I left it two days earlier – in the Aga, a little crispy but not charcoal!

Up early and on the computer. Then off to meet someone at the barn down the lane to sell more hay. Last week, I was panicking about getting rid of last year's harvest. But decided that wasn't going to create desired result, so visualised lots of people contacting me for hay. And? This week, four people phoned and all surplus will be gone by tomorrow. Hurray! Mind-blowing when I make a conscious connection between what I energise and the results.

While at the barn, got talking to the woman who lives there. Solicitor in her late thirties who has seven (yes, seven!) young children, all with biblical names. I love seeing the clothesline strung between two trees when I drive past, embellished with a million pairs of matching socks and other miniature items. As we talk, children are playing in the garden accompanied by a menagerie of animals including goats, pot-bellied pigs, sheep and miniature ponies. It's like a scene out of a children's story book. Says she's ready to go back to work but can't decide what to do. Am I surprised with all that going on? She always wanted a big family and looks fantastic (attractive, slim, bubbly and full of life). Amazing! Obviously has boundless energy if seven kids are no longer using it all up. Impressed.

Back home to check emails before sister and two nephews come for lunch. Then, a horse to ride and back to the barn down the lane to sell more hay. Office makeover is finally complete, so will move furniture back in tonight. It's been very hot today with clear blue skies. Summer solstice means special energy and I'm expecting a brilliant sunset too.

Office set up. What a relief. It looks and feels great. Six colours in all. Quite a spectacle and matches the sunset. Love it and look forward to working in it. Perhaps it's a metaphor for re-booting the business, as well?

Horses done, garden watered. Candlelit bath and so to bed…

Poems

Around the same time as writing the journal, I also started writing poems. One day, I sat down to write a short talk for a family gathering and out popped a poem. It was no effort and took all of a few minutes. And that's how it continued. I wrote poems for my animals, birthday celebrations, work colleagues, the weather and more. It was fun and something I never imagined I could do, though in truth, I hadn't tried. It probably wasn't much different to my approach to writing articles, and I had written hundreds of those. I wrote the first sentence that came into my head on the subject, purposely not thinking too hard about it and the rest flowed from there.

Here are a few of my favourite poems, with a little background to explain each. So, are you sitting comfortably?

On most occasions, when I hosted a large business gathering, I introduced the event with a poem. Admittedly, it was a bit unconventional but I was never one for protocol and I found it created a much more personal connection with the guests. Here is one I wrote and presented at my company's 15th birthday party. The company was a London-based financial planning business for women.

15th Birthday

Birthday girl

Highlights and low-lights there have been
I tell you that to set the scene.

On day one, there was just me
A technical expert and a secretary.
In rooms above the Wigmore Hall
We started off, set out our stall.

Thinking back, all was swell
I had no fear and just as well.
Like a drug, the adrenalin flowed
High as a kite
I must have glowed.

I knew there was a business there
Amongst our sex, so very fair.
My peers laughed
They thought me daft.

But I have shown
With seeds now sewn
That I was right
Evidence, this night.

After a year we moved away
To Savile Row, some time to stay.
We grew and gained a press profile
I was loving it, all the while.

On a mission
With a vision
To empower women about their money
In spite of those who found this funny!

Holistic, service, clear and straight
Those were our watchwords
And it was great,
To make a difference to people's lives
Something to which I always strive.

Covent Garden, next we went
Some 9 years there, we spent.
In two offices by the end
But that did drive us round the bend.

Twenty-five staff at that stage
Sometimes laughter, sometimes rage
At the ups and downs of business life
Its wonders, horrors and its strife.

In dire need of a break
I worked less for a while,
Brought back my smile.
Seventy hours a week or more
Had certainly got to be a bore.

Again, we needed extra space
Room to grow
A leap of faith.
So, we moved again,
This time, it was Ely Place.
Since then, markets have been tough
Business has been tricky, some really testing stuff.

But we are clear about the way
And from our path we will not stray.
Better and better, is what we are dreaming
And we'll get there, kicking or screaming!

Our mantra is unchanged at heart
'Treat others as you would yourself'
This was the essence right from the start.

Alongside running my own independent financial planning business for women, I founded a national non-profit network for women financial advisers. The calendar of events included an annual award scheme to showcase financial women's professionalism to their sceptical male peers, and the public at large. I wrote this for the award dinner in 2003 and read it to some 400 guests.

Come Celebrate With Me

Finalists and me

Come celebrate with me again,
Our 'IFA Women of Achievement'.
Then we'll eat, drink and raise a glass
To our finalists, who are all top class.

They had to go through quite a test
To separate them from the rest.
Grilled for hours at a time,
Compelled to show a pretty good sign
That technically they were sound
And other skills, they had in the 'round'.

Charisma and good with people all,
Balancing work and demands which call
Upon their time, their skills and means
In order to realise their dreams.

All four are worthy indeed.
Words of warning they did not heed,
That the test was tough
In places rough,
Not at all for the faint-hearted.

But once they'd started,
They all coped well,
More than that,
They were swell.

We, as judges did our best
To rise to this most difficult test
In the end we all agreed.
And a unanimous winner was decreed.

So, enjoy this night
By candlelight.
Not long to go,
Before you know.

And for the winner, her year to come
We wish her joy, celebrity and fun.
Make the most of your success
Know for now, that you're the best!

I am a great believer in the power of affirmations and I have used them extensively over the years. They are a superb way to change old patterns of thinking and doing. Old habits die hard and new thoughts, which are the precursor to new skills and behaviours, must be practised until they become our modus operandi. Apart from affirmations written on stickers and stuck to my computer, my desk, my mirror and my car, I also wrote poems as a variation on the theme. Here is one I used to help me overcome debilitating nerves when I went to eventing competitions with my horse. After walking the cross-country course and visualising my approach to every jump and seeing myself coming through the finish safely, I would recite this poem as a finishing touch.

Eventing Invocation

Mares on a mission

Nerves are history
No longer a mystery.
They served me well
Cast a spell,
Which stopped me performing at my best,
Stuck in the crowd with the rest.

Instead, I wish to be in front,
Ahead and more with every jump,
Playing smart in my head,
Nerves in a box, put to bed!

My animals are family. Fanny was a very special cat and a feline 'soul mate'. She lived to the ripe old age of 19 and returned disguised as another cat who possessed her characteristics and behaviours to a tee. He also looked identical. Remarkable! I believe the souls of our dearly beloved animals can return to us, which is something I talk about in a blog in this book.

Fanny's Poem

Fanny

Fanny Adams is my cat
She's magnificent and that's a fact.
She's brown and white
A beautiful sight
With long hair,
Mighty fair.

When we first met
I knew, should I bet,
That this was my girl
My wonderful 'pearl' of a cat
Purrhh, spat, spat!

She follows me around
In the house, without a sound.
She lies while I bath.
It's really quite a laugh,
As by candlelight, late at night,
We two ladies ourselves do clean,
Until we sparkle, shine and gleam.

Then came Benjamin.
At first Fanny had him sussed
He was a pup, so she was brusque.
No nonsense would she stand
She was queen of this fair land.

But Benjamin began to grow,
And one day he did show
His masculinity.
At which point, with some tranquillity
He put her in her place,
And, no, it wasn't in good grace!

Fanny Adams has a sister
Her name is Flossy Cat.
She's frightened of most everything,
There's no disputing that.
They are the opposite in this sense
On two sides of the very same fence.
Fanny loves to be admired
Flossy is shy and retired.

They look the same to the untrained eye
But I know the difference, I can spy
For one has a white nose,
The other is dark
And this is the only way to tell them apart.

Fanny Adams is my cat,
A little overweight but no, not fat.
This is because she prefers the house
To going out 'on the mouse'.
She sits all day in the warmest place
Next to the Aga is her favourite space.

Fanny is fab
And knows me well
She's very good at casting a spell
"Open the door", "Give me my food"
Or, to tick me off if I'm too rude.

Fanny, I love you
You fabulous soul
You add richness to my life
You play a very special role.

My father was 'driven'. He worked relentlessly all his life. He was bright and started with nothing. Through trial and error, he built several businesses. He wasn't easy to live with and, in all honesty, I wasn't either. I had a challenging relationship with him though we made our peace, eventually.

I did an MBA immediately after my undergraduate degree, not because I particularly wanted to but because it was a ticket to London to pursue my sporting ambitions. Secretly, my father was a little envious. When he eventually wound down his business, at the age of 70, after recovering from open heart surgery, he decided to do one to see how business theory compared to the practice. I wrote this poem for his graduation party.

Father Dear

Father dear, you are a star,
I mean what I say,
You truly are.

You went ahead
With your MBA,
Took no heed
Of what I had to say.

And at age 70
You did pass,
With accolades and honours,
Among the best in your class.

Father dear, you are a star
Don't argue with me,
You truly are.

You shine and strive
There's no end to your drive,
Despite two ops
And against the advice of your docs.

Now you can rest
You've done your very best,
And bask in the glory
It is a really great story.

Announce it to all
Better still, have a ball.
It's something to shout about
No doubt, will give you extra clout.

Father dear,
I wish you well,
And what's more, I cast a spell
"To *take time and enjoy life's pleasures,*
No longer judge yourself in weights and measures."

You've proved to everyone, all around,
That in intellect and stamina,
You abound.

Stand tall, head high,
You are worthy indeed,
Joe Price has an MBA,
Official, it is decreed!

I believe the elements have consciousness and that we can connect with them. After all, Mother Earth is our biological parent and the elements are one of her systems. So, this is an invocation asking the weather to be kind for hay making. I used invocations in other weather situations too. For example, in dangerous conditions when I wanted the eye of the storm to pass me by. Or, if I was competing at a horse show and needed a short break from horizontal rain or gales. Invariably, my requests were granted. I believe this type of communication can work when it's done respectfully and honours the fact that local weather can only be redirected if it doesn't create a danger nearby. Weather is a system, not an isolated event and local changes will have knock-on effects elsewhere.

Hay Making Ode

Weather be fine
Nothing short of divine.
Sun, shine your rays
So we can make hay.

England at its best
Excels all the rest,
Land so fair
Know we care.

Help me now
You know how.
I honour you well
Cast your spell!

Biz-Chat

After I sold my women's financial business in 2004, I promised myself that I was done with business – as far as starting and growing one was concerned. I had had my nose to the grindstone, barely coming up for air, since graduating 20 years previously and I desperately needed a change. I also felt sure it would be easier to manage a business of one, namely me.

During the next few years, I held a number of non-executive directorships, alongside consultancy and mentoring. But as it turned out, I hadn't quite finished with business or championing the role of women. My experience of working with women and advocating for them in the financial sector was still omnipresent.

For a number of years, I had wanted to work in broadcast. But trying to break into the mainstream was challenging and when an opening finally occurred, existing business commitments prevented me from taking it up. Now, though, there was a window of opportunity. Video was the new thing on the web, so I could become a content creator. In 2008, I came up with the idea of launching a subscription website to showcase women's leadership style on video and provide a space for them to share their experiences (social media didn't exist then). Oh, how quickly I had forgotten the pain, not to mention the cost, of getting a new venture off the ground!

In between filming interviews with 100 or so leading UK businesswomen in the first 12 months of the 'Diva-Biz' website, I recorded a few of my own business insights. Here are some of the transcripts of those 'Biz-Chats'.

Women don't sell

Many women think that *selling* is a dirty word. At worst it has a connotation of persuasion, convincing people they need something they don't and implies manipulation or intimidation. Generally, women have a very different selling style to men, and selling a service, which is my area of experience, is actually something we do very well.

This is because it's important that we believe in what we do, as our prime motive isn't usually money, status or power. It's also because we take personal responsibility for the consequences of our actions, so we need to feel we are doing the right thing for our clients. And it's because we understand the emotions underlying our clients' behaviour, which enables us to address their concerns and create a bond of trust, which is so important in service-based businesses.

In addition, we value relationships which we build over time and which help us to secure repeat business with clients, as well as retain staff – a virtuous circle, as staff retention aids client retention. In time, perhaps the definition of *selling* will change and maybe even the word, to reflect the idea of an exchange taking place between a business and its clients which is honest, open and mutually beneficial.

Truth in business

There is no such thing as the truth in business. People come to each situation with their own rose-tinted spectacles according to their experiences, expectations and baggage. That's why there is so much disagreement. It's hugely important to understand the perspective other people bring so you don't carry hurt, grief or anger away from conflict. When disagreement ends this way, somebody will feel aggrieved and, if it's you, it will be a drag factor on your performance and wellbeing, in the future.

I am not suggesting you should be a saint and forgive everything people do which is hurtful or creates anger. What I am suggesting is that, for your own self-preservation, you try to understand why people think and act the way they do, so you can let it go. This avoids carrying negative emotion into your future as, the chances are, it will eventually make you ill, unhappy or both. It just doesn't work. Forgiveness can follow later *if* you want to go the extra mile, which will stop your energy being sapped by the residue of past events.

Standing out from the crowd

Why do some people stand out more than others? Well, as a woman in a man's world, it goes without saying that you have to be especially good at what you do in order to succeed. But over and above that, it's also about expressing your individuality – how you dress, your views, your character, your beliefs and even your quirks.

Most of us don't have the confidence to do this when we start out in business, I certainly didn't. Instinctively, we tone down in order to blend in. Or we use props like clothes to support us and give us confidence rather than to express who we really are. The first suit I ever bought was navy because it helped me feel authoritative when I was seeing a new client or giving a talk.

But in time, we need to be more of who we are, not less. True charisma comes from unabashed originality and authenticity, ie it is aligned to our values and walking our talk. It's about being the unique individual we truly are and not being afraid to show it. It's compelling, it's easy to recognise and connect with and it's the mark of a leader, and those who stand out from the crowd. It also creates a powerful energy that touches the consciousness of those who come into contact with it and acts as a source of inspiration.

Oddly enough, smiling makes a big impact too. Research has shown that children smile about 300 times a day, whereas adults only manage a measly 27 smiles. But it's a valuable habit to develop, as adults who smile generate 4 times more business! Similarly, presenters who smile are rated much higher than those who don't. It's no wonder then, that when you are doing a talk your delivery style counts for a massive 90%, and the message a mere 10%. When I start a talk, I often forget to smile because I am concentrating on the message. So, I draw a 'smiley' on the top of each page to remind me.

Developing your individuality and authenticity in business is as important as learning conventional skills such as time management and negotiation skills, yet it doesn't even get a mention in business education. People who have the courage to do this stand out from the crowd and, in my opinion, it's one of the secret ingredients of success.

Good ideas

I think the biggest misconception about good ideas is that they come fully formed with bells and whistles on right from the start, and are crystal clear. They aren't. Most good ideas start small. A little seed of an idea – blink and you miss it. But if you give it time and start to embellish it, the seed can quickly grow to the point where it becomes omnipresent and you think 'Wow', this could really be something.

I look back to when I started my first long-term business. I had just finished university where there were a broadly similar number of men and women, and found myself in the financial world where there were virtually no women at all. So, I joined 'Women in...' everything I could find (management, business, property, the City and more) in search of a female peer group. This was at the start of the businesswomen's networking movement in London in the early '80s.

Gradually, as I attended regular events, I was asked for financial advice by some of the other members and a tiny thought occurred to me, namely, that it could be fun to start a woman-to-woman business because women approached their finances with different 'stuff' to men. So, I began to think about it. I imagined how it might be, the PR possibilities and what it would be like to work exclusively with women as staff and clients. I stumbled across information that was useful and which created more ideas on the theme. The vision grew and, one day, I got to the point where I thought, "This is a really good idea and I am just going to do it". So, from a very small seed, the idea became so big and tangible that I could feel myself in the space. It had become my alternative reality and there was really no decision to be made.

The other thing about good ideas is that they are often new and untried, so you have to be prepared to go against convention. Basically, after doing your research and honing your vision, you may have to keep it to yourself while you start planning. Others won't have the same vision and passion as you do and could well be discouraging. In my case, the type of responses I got were, "There aren't enough potential women clients" or "Finances are the same for men and women so it isn't a niche business idea". I quickly realised I needed to keep my own counsel to avoid negativity. In the end, I proved the idea was good by making it a success. If you discuss your big idea was good with someone else, be highly selective. In my experience, the best time for taking advice is in executing the plan.

One final thought. Passion is powerful in business. It means it won't feel like work (a big plus when you are likely to spend so much time doing it). You will also draw people to you who share your passion, which makes work a joy.

Surround yourself with the right people

It's critically important in business to surround yourself with the right people. This is something I have learned to my cost several times over. Obviously, when you are recruiting you need to find people who can do the job. But if those people don't share your goals, vision and outlook, you will spend a lot of time and energy lining people up and pointing them in the same direction, with little energy left to create momentum in the business. It will be a constant process of two steps forward and one step back, which is tiring and expensive.

Conversely, if you surround yourself with people who are on the same wavelength, you will barely need to communicate your values, so moving the business forwards is easy and fun. People energise each other and the result is bigger than the sum of the parts.

Similarly, it's important to surround yourself with the right sources of information. You simply can't know everything. This was especially true for me in a constantly changing financial world. Interestingly, women in finance are often more qualified than their male peers because they don't like to have a meeting with clients and not know the answers. Nonetheless, we all need people we can call on, from time to time, for expert information, whether they are inside or outside your organisation. Furthermore, we have to be brave enough to ask what seem like 'silly' questions and insist that the answers come back in plain English, no matter how complex the subject matter. In fact, this is a key skill in life – knowing what questions to ask, where to go for the information and persisting until you understand.

The best you can be

Almost everything in business for me, is encapsulated in the idea of being the best you can be. If you don't work on this then you won't realise your potential, or that of your business. Business is a classroom. It's an opportunity to learn how to manage yourself and become a 'business athlete'. You can begin by noticing what you do, ie what works, what doesn't and how you feel about it. Then, as with all things you want to improve, it's a question of honing your skill. Practice makes perfect. Or, more precisely, 'perfect practice makes perfect'!

Here are a few examples of skills I have consciously worked at. The first is *presentations*. Many of us have had the experience of being incredibly nervous about public speaking. You get up to speak and you wish the floor would swallow you up. Your throat is dry, you are short of breath and a tiny pipsqueak of a voice emerges from the top of your lungs. Not a good start. You have just 20 seconds to make an impression and it needs to be a good one.

Actors and actresses are taught to do physical exercise as well as a vocal warm-up before going on stage. I found I needed a combination of mental and physical preparation. Firstly, I would remind myself I was there because I knew more than the audience about my subject (even though I didn't consider myself to be an expert, as they did). Secondly, I would dash off to the Ladies (or any quiet corner I could find) to do some stretching and a few press-ups, to ensure my physical body was relaxed by the time I got up to speak. Then my voice and I would be operating at full power from the first word. Unless you are an experienced speaker, the chances are you will need to prepare in one way or another to maximise your impact. Do what you have to!

Another example is *increasing your personal effectiveness* in order to perform better when you have a busy schedule. Most of my office days were packed with back-to-back meetings, punctuated by the odd half an hour for other tasks. So, my preparation began the moment I got out of bed. Before I did anything else, I would sit quietly and imagine the day. I visualised finishing each meeting feeling pleased it had gone well, or being happy with the presentation I had written in the slot between meetings. Basically, I set myself up at an energy level to achieve all the tasks in my schedule, before I even got dressed or stepped out of the house.

A third example is *decision-making*. A full-on day at the office is not a good place to make important business decisions. There are too many distractions and too much multi-tasking going on. So, I created a discipline around making decisions and used the time in between things, like commuting. For a number of years, the journey home was the time that I developed my thinking on issues which had arisen during the day and, if possible, make a decision by the time I arrived at my front door.

This meant there were occasions when I sat on the doorstep until I had reached a satisfactory point in my thinking – which must have seemed very strange to my neighbours! I would also use the journey from my house to my horses several times a week. This practice created a structure around decision-making which improved outcomes enormously. It also allowed me to switch off in the small amount of personal time I had in my life.

The power of change

Change is a given. We must accept it is one of the constants in life. We just don't always see it coming. The feeling of being uncomfortable with something fundamental such as work, relationships, our home or our financial situation is a clue that something needs to change. But we fear the unknown or believe we don't have any options. We feel stuck and out of control. Consequently, we stay in this negative space for too long and the further down the slippery slope we slide, the harder it is to crawl out.

Processing the situation and being honest with ourselves, is the starting point. Honesty brings clarity and clarity illuminates previously unseen options. We feel better when we begin to take control back, and move away from uncertainty. Once we decide on a course of action, things are definitely on the up and we can begin to plan our way forwards. Focusing on creating a new situation is positive and empowering and a sense of momentum returns to our life.

The trick for reducing the pain of change is to recognise the tell-tale signs as early as possible and understand the process. Change is something we need to engage with, as it's the quickest form of learning there is. It also brings new opportunities to trigger our creative juices. In my longest-standing business of 18 years, the changes I least wanted to make (which were also the most scary) turned out to be opportunities that renewed my interest and gave rise to new projects.

For instance, after 10 relentless years getting the business off the ground, I was burned out and forced to think about work-life balance. I moved out of London to the countryside. This gave me a chance to renovate a period property (which was enjoyable) and have a different focus for a while . Also, I was finally able to keep my horses at home. But by moving away from London, I couldn't be in the office all the time and had to work from home several days a week. This felt uncomfortable to start with, as I was paranoid about the consequences of not leading from the front, or being visible. But it turned out to be a good move because it refreshed my appetite for business. Meanwhile, colleagues stepped up to take the helm which taught me to delegate. This was a bonus when it came to selling the business because I had proved it could work without me.

What is instinct?

Instinct is like internal 'sat-nav'. When you are connected to it you are prompted to go here or there, do this or that at precisely the right time, so that you make an important business connection or find the information you need. Basically, instinct guides you through the hazards of life far more quickly than logic, to get you where you want to go. It doesn't cost anything, and you don't have to go on a course. You just need to pay attention to how you feel and learn to be balanced. When you are balanced, you have full access to your instinct and are connected with the 'field of possibilities'. Then, through synchronicity, you will attract what you want, assuming it's what you are focused on.

Being balanced also allows you to be fully present in each business situation, so you can take in information at all levels, including what is spoken and what is not. This increases your awareness (think of it as 'situational instinct') which helps you to make better decisions. In time, you will notice more quickly when you are out of balance and develop ways to get back there. Definitely, avoid making decisions when you are unbalanced because they will invariably be the ones you live to regret!

Working excessively

I am probably not alone in having justified excessive working hours over many years, on the grounds that I am building something for the future. This gave me permission to work flat out today, tomorrow, this weekend and this year, for what I might achieve in 2, 3, 5 or 10-years' time. Thankfully, I have come to my senses. I realised that by the time I got there, what I was striving for wouldn't be as meaningful and, even if it was, I wouldn't know how to appreciate it because stopping to appreciate things is not something I knew how to do.

The pattern of excessive working and delayed gratification means you give yourself a hard time, lots of stress, possibly ill-health and miss out on some great adventures along the way, by being so fixed on one course. Hard work is great when it gives you a buzz. The buzz means you are in your sweet spot and you are highly effective. But I no longer do 'it' to the exclusion of everything else because there have to be things, even small things, every day which make life richer and more meaningful.

Does success equal happiness?

Success has long been associated with money, status and power. But you only have to look around you at the people who have these things to see that it doesn't always create a nirvana for them. A better measure, I think, is happiness. If success equals happiness, then it's as individual as each of us. And if you can't define it by its outward appearance, then what does it feel like?

Well, for me (and I can only talk for myself), it's when your life is an inspiration, and you pass the gift of inspiration to others. It's when work isn't toil because it's passion. It's when you are true to yourself and those around you. It's when you have the courage to act, when you have faith and not control, when you believe in yourself and know you are not alone because there is also divine intervention.

One of my business school lecturers said about ethics – "You can't define it but you know it when you see it". I think happiness is the same. You recognise it in yourself and others.

Learning to be a 'business athlete'

Talks

Between 2000 and 2004, during the last few years of my London business phase, I was frequently invited to speak at events – mostly to business women but not always. Some of my talks fleshed out themes from the 'Biz-Chat' transcripts. I would like to share them with you, as they epitomize my rather 'unconventional' approach to business. It was challenging to find the courage to speak my truth, in a business world that had barely discovered the term 'emotional intelligence'. But being considered successful gave me some latitude which I used to the full.

This first piece is just the introduction to a talk I gave to a women's network in 2001. I have included it because it sums up the context for what follows:

Introduction

One of the stand-out benefits of being an entrepreneur is having the freedom to make things up as you go along and be the orchestrator of your own experience. For me, business has been an incredible classroom, far better than any business school (I know, I went) especially if you are starting a company from scratch and are a naive and enthusiastic beginner, with no frame of reference – which is just as well!

In trying to understand the many, often challenging (in the extreme) experiences I have encountered, I have been fascinated by the personal, emotional and spiritual dynamics which are present in all situations. Understanding myself and others to the best of my ability and the contribution all participants make to every situation (especially the tricky ones) is a fascination which has consumed me for as long as I can remember.

The net effect of this as a speaker is that I am very focused on that all-elusive 'secret ingredient x'. How can we be all we want to be, have all we dream of and make a difference to the world?

It occurred to me early on in my business life that technical knowledge probably accounts for less than half the total outcome. A proportion of the rest is down to tangible skills such as organizational ability, time management, communication (verbal and non-verbal), strategic planning and delegation, and the remainder is based on subtle skills which are about how you handle yourself.

Technical training is readily available, while the subtle stuff is hardly even talked about, let alone taught. Yet it makes all the difference, not only to success but to happiness, as well.

Subtle skills are practical and essential (in business and in life) and include things such as how you pick yourself up off the floor when your world caves in, how you recognize when you are sliding down the slippery slope, how you resolve conflict, cope with pressure, make decisions, spot opportunities, stay balanced, reduce stress and build belief in yourself.

I certainly don't have all the answers as this is a lifetime's quest, and more. But I'd like to share a few of the insights with you, that I have gained along the way.

This talk was given to members of a prestigious UK financial institute in 2002. I was speaking to a male audience. No surprise, as there were only around 1500 women in the entire financial planning sector at the time, and I was usually the token woman in the room, whether or not I was the speaker! Little did the audience of pin-striped gents know I was about to deliver my alternative perspective on business life. To put the talk into context, there had been a stock market crisis that year and more trouble was brewing. But I had my own business crisis going on too.

'Stuff'

An alternative take on the business of finance

What stuff? I didn't have anything particular in mind when I was asked what I would like to talk about and I randomly uttered the word 'Stuff'. I was surrounded by it, immersed in it and it was occupying much of my attention at the time. I couldn't think of anything better to talk about, so the title stuck. The good news is that it offers plenty of scope to talk about all manner of weird and wonderful things which are largely undefined, untaught and certainly underestimated. Things that I come across in my everyday life and which I expect you do too. I call these things 'under the skin' factors. They are irritants and intangible, but they usually make all the difference between success and failure, and quality of life.

'Stuff' comes in many different shapes and sizes; there's sticky stuff, fluffy stuff, mucky stuff, slushy stuff, juicy stuff, jolly stuff and jolly weird stuff among other varieties, or you can 'pick and mix' your own! So, we'll start with some **sticky stuff**. What type of age are we living and working in? It's certainly fast and furious. So much seems to have happened in such a short time – economically, politically, professionally and, for me, personally.

Ironically, change is something most of us resist if we possibly can, yet it is a constant in life, so much so that time itself is speeding up. The industrial revolution took us 100 years but it will only take China 10. Today's computer is more powerful than all the computers put together in the '50s and the power of computers is doubling every year. And I don't know whether you've noticed but many younger people seem to be so wise, so young. Certainly, they often leave me with my jaw gaping at some of the profundities they come out with (even my nephews who are under the age of 5). Globally, of course, thanks to rapid advances in telecommunications, we are very aware of the incredible pace of change, from disasters to space age innovation.

The problem with change is that you cannot be certain what's on the other side of it. It's about the unknown. In the case of big life changes, we often feel powerless, as we view ourselves to be the victim of circumstances. We feel out of control. Usually, however (at least to start), we are totally unaware that change is in the air; we just feel frustrated and uneasy about things and consequently we put off bringing this semi-conscious feeling into conscious thought, so we can deal with it. Instead, we wallow around in our discomfort and become negative about practically everything.

It's impossible for us mere mortals to live in a constantly positive state, after all, it's our fallibility that makes us human. But it is possible to minimise the time we spend being negative if we are observant, as *sticky* stuff has a nasty habit of creeping up on us.

In my own life, I have learned to recognise that a prolonged uneasy feeling means that change is highly likely. Whether I choose to change or not is another matter but, the point is, I have an opportunity to examine what isn't working. The first step in bringing the problem into consciousness is to examine all causes of unease. At this point, we are still living with uncertainty, as we don't know what we're going to do. So we can't expect to feel too much better.

Having identified the prime cause though, we can look at options. Rule nothing out, no matter how absurd or ridiculous. Many a dream-come-true started with some frivolous idea or other, that came out of the devastation of life as we knew it. Once we make a conscious decision about what to change (or not to change), we can bounce back. Why? Because we are in control of our lives again.

Deepak Chopra, a writer combining the scientific and esoteric, summed it up by saying: "The known is our past. The known is nothing other than the prison of past conditioning. There's no evolution in that – absolutely none at all. And when there is no evolution, there is stagnation, entropy, disorder, and decay. Uncertainty, on the other hand, is the fertile ground of pure creativity and freedom."

A word of caution, however, which brings me to some **fluffy stuff**, namely instinct (the male version) and intuition (the female version). Having considered the different options, I then chew things over for a while and live with each possibility in my imagination to see how it feels.

By doing this I am testing my intuition (that thing of no fixed abode) which past experience tells me is far more reliable than logic. Logic says "do such and such" because it is less risky, or it's what you can afford, or it's more convenient and, let's face it, it's more tangible because it's probably sitting on a piece of paper in front of you. But that doesn't make it right. In fact, logic could be leading you down a blind alley.

Conversely, instinct, our innate mechanism for accessing the bigger picture, is something we are born with but we forget it exists, let alone how to use it. This isn't surprising in a society which values intellectual prowess and academic training much more highly. We have an instinct in every situation but it dissolves in a flash as we intellectualise it away. So, we have to learn to recognise instinct and hold on to it long enough to examine it. I pay attention to the feeling in my gut. Do I feel comfortable with the idea and relaxed in my gut, no matter how mad it seems on paper? Or do I feel a knot in the pit of my stomach? That is instinct and the best decisions are made 'instinct first, logic second'. Instinct to decide the course of action and logic for planning.

Surprisingly, when I have gone with my gut feel (which often requires a considerable leap of faith) there has been a happy ending. And when I've gone against it – well, I'll skip that bit! It sounds the easiest thing in the world, to follow your instinct. I haven't always chosen the easy option, that's for sure. However, I understand my process now and by owning up to the feeling of impending doom (the fog that pre-empts change), I know I can minimise the pain and make the change that's waiting for me, quicker – if, that is, I can deal with the 'F' factor.

'F' stands for fear. This is the **mucky stuff**. Fear is the greatest single inhibitor for all of us. Even when we know intuitively what the best solution is, we can still freeze and fail to act – 'rabbit in the headlights' syndrome. The only way to overcome fear is to tackle it head-on and find out what the absolute worst scenario is. Usually, it's about loss of material things such as money or property, or it can be loss of face (though that's unlikely to make you destitute). We carry our true riches inside and whatever you've achieved once, you can do again.

So, if by acting on instinct your business could face financial ruin (a worst scenario based on what is known), what's the bottom line – an end to your world? Or would you be able to find a well-paid job working for someone else, at least in the meantime?

Believe me, I've tested the 'what-if' scenarios many times and when you reach the ultimate 'what-if' and find it isn't life-threatening, it's amazingly liberating. Only then do you realise how much energy you've wasted on worry and avoidance. But don't just believe me, try it for yourself and chance the option that feels good.

Fear is devious; sometimes the truth of the matter is the opposite to what we think, which makes the 'F-factor' very difficult to detect. For example, fear of our personal power or even fear of success could be what immobilises us, not the fear of failure, as we might think. These words, by Marianne Williamson, were made famous by Nelson Mandela in his inaugural speech in 1992. They sum it up:

"Our deepest fear is not that we are inadequate. Our deepest fear is that we are powerful beyond measure. It is our light, not our darkness that most frightens us. We ask ourselves, 'Who am I to be brilliant, gorgeous, talented, fabulous?' Actually, who are you not to be? You are a child of God. Your playing small does not serve the world. There is nothing enlightened about shrinking so that other people won't feel insecure around you. We are all meant to shine, as children do. We were born to make manifest the glory of God that is within us. It's not just in some of us; it's in everyone. And as we let our own light shine, we unconsciously give other people permission to do the same. As we are liberated from our own fear, our presence automatically liberates others."

I've talked about how to recognise the need for change and what to do about it. But it can take time to replace ingrained habits of thinking and doing and become skilled at the art of change. I am sure we've all met people who have a repeating pattern, which they are oblivious to. "Why does she always go for that type of man? It'll end in tears, again" (the *slushy* stuff). "He's so good at recruiting people but he's a hopeless manager and loses as many as he recruits" (the *slimy* stuff). What's your 'repeater'? We all have them.

Onto the **juicy stuff**. Once is enough for me! My new motto is 'Baggage-free travel'. When things appear to go wrong, I try not to get too depressed about it and re-live the experience over and over again; this doesn't mean I'm ecstatic about it either. But I want to get to the bottom of it so I can learn what I need to know, to avoid getting into the same situation again. I believe there is meaning in everything. Life is full of clues which tell us valuable things about ourselves and how we behave in every situation.

This requires reflection. It can take days, weeks or sometimes, years. We must do our best to understand what part we played in an interaction that caused grief (without letting our ego get in the way) and decide if we acted properly or not. We also need to think about the part others played and why. This means putting ourselves in other people's shoes and trying to see the world from their perspective.

We all see things differently. Consequently, there can be many versions of the truth, which means each person acts according to their own particular rose-tinted spectacles. Reality is an interpretation coloured by our experience, fears, expectations, personality and more. Realising this is an eye-opener. It enables us to stop being frustrated with people for not being clones of ourselves, and even begin to value their differences and uniqueness. We realise that, in most cases, people don't act out of malice, they simply do what they believe is right.

Sometimes then, the conclusion is that no one was wrong, we just failed to recognise our differences and appreciate that everyone was trying to do the best from their perspective. *Deepak Chopra said, "Every so-called upsetting situation will become an opportunity for the creation of something new and beautiful and every so-called tormentor or tyrant will become your teacher."*

Personally, I need to understand somebody else's perspective before I can move on without bearing a grudge. I think we greatly underestimate the damage that bitterness and resentment does to our health – physically, mentally and emotionally. Constantly searching for truth and attempting to live it, is an enormous challenge but it's preferable to living in 'guilt' or 'hurt', which is responsible for much unhappiness and probably illness. Life without insights would be unthinkable, wouldn't it?

Let's take a look at the **dreamy stuff** – aspiration and inspiration. Many times, I have been disillusioned about working in the financial sector, given the amount of mis-selling and unethical practices; many times I've been completely frustrated by the bureaucracy of regulation; many times I've been exhausted by simply trying to do it well and have wished I could be anywhere else.

But what has kept me here and what has motivated me, is that I believe in what I am doing and am inspired by it (working with women) and I aspire to do my work with excellence. We have a tremendous responsibility to make a positive difference to people's lives through effective management of the 'life-blood' of our industry, which is money. Moreover, our job is special because people have to take us on faith and won't see the results of our work, sometimes for years. In my business, I also believe I am playing an important part in women's empowerment through the confidence and security that financial independence brings.

Inspiration is food for the soul so, we have a duty to find ways of remaining inspired because if we don't, we are of little use to anyone (colleagues, clients, friends, family or ourselves) and should change our job. Sai Baba, acclaimed as a present-day prophet, summed it up by saying: "It is the heart that reaches the goal. Follow the heart, for a pure heart seeks beyond the intellect – it gets inspired." By following our heart, I believe we will find our area of excellence, the place where we can shine, be fulfilled and make a contribution to the world around us.

The financial world has a bad reputation and I have no qualms about saying it is deserved because, in the past, there has been considerable bad practice. Sadly, despite many changes in recent years, there is still a cancer in our community, though perhaps it's less obvious. If we are inspired about what we do, we should stand up and be counted and help to bring about change, by voicing our opinions and demonstrating best practice. In small ways we can all make a difference.

It is up to us, not the regulators, journalists or anyone else, to change the financial world into one which is trusted, respected and credited with the importance it deserves in helping people to become financially secure. If this seems like an overwhelming prospect, it only takes one person to strike a match in a dark room for a light to shine. That's the power we have to change our world.

So, on to group transformation, the **jolly stuff**. This starts at an individual level, ie getting our own house in order. It begins with a search for personal truth (the **mysterious stuff**) and there are no quick fixes here. Being true to yourself means not settling for second best. And to create organisational change (which is a catalyst for wider cultural change), means everyone in the work environment, from the top person to the office junior, must be engaged in the idea of upping their game and doing their best.

I admit I am a perfectionist and I have been criticised for this in the past. But I make no excuses for it. I think it's only because mediocrity is the norm that aspiring to excellence appears to be extreme, even to ourselves, at times. Of course, on occasion, you have to temper perfectionism with practical constraints (the **tedious stuff**)!

Basing a business on integrity is not the most profitable option. You do it because you believe in it. But it is possible to be fairly paid for your efforts, and the satisfaction you get from seeing the difference you make to people is priceless. Part of the problem in the financial sector, is that there are still some who measure themselves by '80s standards and are trying to perpetuate past income levels. To be blunt, I think the sector was overpaid then and still is. It isn't (as I so often hear people say) that we have to work harder for less. This is the real world. To make sustainable progress, we have to downgrade our expectation of returns, just as we have asked our clients to downgrade their investment expectations.

It has been said, *"The past is history, the future is a mystery and the moment is a gift. That is why this moment is called the present"*. Wonderful, isn't it? Of course, we all get wrapped up in planning for the future but, equally, it's easy to get hooked on living in the past. We must find time to be centred in the present and see what's here right now, and appreciate it, appreciate ourselves and the world around us, as this puts a different slant on everything.

Being in the moment is an essential part of creating the future (the **weird stuff**). *"Attention energises and intention transforms"*. Attention is about noticing. This is something we can only do when we are centred in the moment. So, how do we energise our attention to create the future we want? We use our mind to focus on what we want in a committed and joyful way, seeing and sensing it as if it is already manifested. Meditation is a good way to train the mind to be focused. There are health benefits too, apart from creating a greater sense of calm amidst the storm of life.

Interestingly, we use the power of the mind to manifest things whether we realise it or not. For instance, when we think of someone and they get in touch, or we bump into them in the street. But we can use it in more purposeful ways too, in our business and personal life.

Thought is an energy form and, as such, it has a cause-and-effect relationship with the world around us. If our thoughts are strong enough and consistent, they become the engine of creation. Like any new skill, this requires practice. One way to practise is on your body (the **very weird stuff**), to aid healing. I've found that if I accidentally cut myself, I can stop the bleeding or reduce bruising, and speed up the healing process. To stop bleeding, I just imagine the blood turning into treacle and clotting. I then create a vivid image, such as an army of little people knitting the skin back together. Or I look at a piece of skin that's undamaged and superimpose the mental image of that over the wound. Any or all of the above act as instructions to the body to repair itself and it innately knows how to do this.

Similarly, I use my mind to control pain when I am injured. Our immediate reaction is to hold onto pain and tense up in an effort to minimise it. But this achieves the opposite and it lasts for longer. Instead, if you relax into the pain and experience it fully, it crescendos and then subsides. This feels like a big wave washing over you (which isn't as bad as you think) leaving far less residual pain, and allowing you to start the process of visualisation and healing. I have done it many times and each time, to my amazement, it works.

The most dramatic example was when I amputated the end of my finger in an accident 18 months ago. This was a real test for me. I managed to stop the bleeding and anaesthetise the pain using mental instructions I gave to my body. My finger was stitched back on and healed with imperceivable scarring, no infection and no loss of function.

Don't believe me, try it for yourself. Though there is no need to be so dramatic. Start with a scratch or a bruise! Exercising mental muscles you never knew you had and seeing tangible results in your body will give you the confidence to experiment with the power of thought in other areas of your life too.

So, what does all this 'stuff' add up to? Well, if we're adding up, we're talking numbers – back to what we know and love in the financial world. But not so fast! I thought I'd consult numerology. Each letter of the word STUFF has a corresponding number, the total of which is 9. What is the significance of the number 9? Well, as it happens nine is the number of completion. This could relate to a phase in our lives, or a phase for humanity. Either way, completion inevitably leads to change and new beginnings. So, perhaps by focusing on our 'stuff' and gaining mastery over ourselves, we can create the change we want in our lives, in the world around us and in the financial world too.

*I gave this talk to a businesswomen's network in the Midlands in 2001.
My working life had been crazy from the start (London-based and I was
18 years into my long-term business at this point), which focused my
thinking on personal survival strategies on a daily basis.*

The ultimate relationship

Sport was an excellent grounding for business, for me

I imagine that everyone here, one way or the other, is in search of
the ultimate relationship. For the avoidance of doubt, that's the
one with yourself! I suspect there isn't a person in the room who
doesn't want to be a better version of themselves. However, you
have to know who you are first.

Oddly enough, who we think we are is usually tied up with who other people think we are (or want us to be), namely our family, friends and colleagues. So, we grow up relying on external validation for our identity and self-esteem. As a result, we go through life feeling we aren't always in control and, all too often, that we are a victim of circumstances. Sadly, if we look around, this approach to life appears to be normal.

Being the creator of our own experience is the exact opposite. It requires us to start with what's inside and work outwards. If we can discover who we really are by learning to be conscious of our thoughts and behaviours, we can amplify what we like and minimise what we don't like. But this idea is rarely understood, let alone taught. So, it's down to each of us to embark on a voyage of personal discovery, if we choose to. Discovering who we are and working on becoming more of who we want to be, is a game-changer. In my life, it has brought a sense of magic, greater peace and the realisation that I am a powerful creator.

Let me explain some of the formative influences that led me to this way of thinking. I've always lived life at full throttle with a 'bring it on' attitude and, unsurprisingly, this has brought constant challenge and change which has massively accelerated my learning and taught me so much. Challenging as it has been, I wouldn't have it any other way.

In my teens and early twenties, I was a Welsh rowing international which was a fantastic grounding for business, as it happens. Rowing is a ridiculously tough sport and I learned that performance is a blend of the raw material you start with plus technical skills you learn and hone, your physical strength, ultra-fitness, stamina, endless practice, courage, belief in yourself, inspiration, mental focus, nutrition, teamwork, lifestyle and more. This is pretty much the same recipe for success in any sphere. So, in my working life, I decided to think of myself as a 'business athlete' to help me create a framework for identifying the areas I needed to work on, in order to up my game.

Before university, I spent a year on the other side of the world, in Australia, working and travelling on my own. Mobile phones and the internet hadn't been invented then, so I really was alone. That was a big initiation. Boy, did I quickly learn how to 'read' people, be resourceful, trust myself and be brave.

University followed and I'm not sure what a psychology degree taught me, except perhaps to be aware that "all is not what it seems". Actually, that's quite important. Business school came next and it was a huge disappointment. It was ultra-academic and not at all helpful in starting a business from scratch. Grandiose marketing models may work in big corporations but they were of no use to me, when I started out on an overdraft of £10,000 and discovered that 'cashflow was king'.

One useful by-product of business school, however, was that I came away thinking I was the only MBA graduate who couldn't read a balance sheet! This set me up very nicely for the business I am in now, where plain communication in financial matters counts for a lot. In fact, one of the reasons I set up this business was that I discovered a lack of confidence around figures was common to many women, particularly the 30+ generation. It stems from social conditioning, ie the attitude "I'll be taken care of". Yes, for all the gains we've made, this still lurks in our collective female psyche! It's also a result of poor maths teaching coupled with programming that "maths isn't a girl's subject". This leads many women to choose non-mathematical degrees and jobs and avoid getting involved in the finances in their personal relationships, too.

The other main by-product of my business education was that I knew I was unemployable. Many on my course had worked in big corporations and, from what they told me, I knew I wouldn't like taking orders or playing politics. I wanted to make my experience up each day, act on my own instincts and be the master of my destiny.

So, within three years of leaving business school, I set up my first business with a friend. Starting with a blank piece of paper is exciting, fun, challenging and scary. You invent it as you go, live on your wits and find courage you never knew you had. It takes tenacity, resourcefulness and hard graft. Of course, it isn't for everyone and it's one of those things you don't know you can pull off, until you do.

We raised £25,000 from a private investor (banks weren't an option as we had no experience), recruited 8 people and found premises during the Christmas of 1986 in the midst of a BT strike (and there was no option other than BT then). However, I soon discovered that my partner and I didn't see eye to eye on some key issues and I realised that you don't really know someone in business until a contractual relationship binds you. It was a hard lesson to learn.

I left after 2 years to set up my current company. I was 28 and entering the fifth year of my working life. The great thing about youth is that you learn fast and bounce back well. I was eager for more.

When I entered the financial world in 1983, I was shocked to find there were almost no women. So, I joined a number of business and professional women's networks which were getting started in the early '80s, in order to find a female peer group. Participating in these networks gave me the idea to launch a 'woman to woman' financial business, in spite of ridicule from men in the sector. I think I got the last laugh!

I set up in a couple of converted piano practice rooms over the Wigmore Hall in London, with two staff. After a year we moved to bigger premises in Savile Row and 18 months later, we moved into our own building in Covent Garden. This expanded to two buildings over the next 9 years and then we moved to double the space in the City to accommodate a staff of 30 and give us room to grow.

Although there have been monumental challenges along the way, I have always been passionate about empowering women through financial independence, because money brings choices. This has given me the energy and commitment to persevere, even in the darkest moments. Passion about your business is vital, for this and other reasons.

Over the last 13 years, my role in the business has changed. The first time, it involved moving away from client work into PR and marketing, so I could raise the company's profile and attract new clients. This was risky as I was the main client manager but it was essential. I knew nothing about dealing with the press, writing articles or PR but I loved building relationships with the media and appearing on programmes like *Woman's Hour, The Today Programme, News at Ten* and others. I learned what the media wanted in order to be useful and being a token woman in a man's world, for once, proved to be an advantage. When you are introduced as an expert (which is not how I think of myself), you have to be extremely well prepared and quick-thinking if the conversation goes 'off-piste'. It's testing but great fun.

By my mid-thirties, I was jaded and needed time away from the business. I'd been working without a break for years, putting in 70 hours a week and I was tired – not something I could easily admit to. So, I recruited a marketing manager and forced myself to drop down to 4 days a week (albeit guilt-ridden). Then to three days.

A bit later, I moved out of London to ensure I didn't slip back to working full-time and bought a house with land that needed renovation and adapting to accommodate me and my horses. This put the pressure on to reduce my days in the office to just two, while I managed the project at home, which lasted 18 months.

It was a difficult time. On the one hand, I was experiencing the joy of something creative again. But on the other hand, the business wasn't going so well without me at the helm and problems had arisen that I didn't want to face. Eventually, things came to a head and I had to bite the bullet and go back to working full-time, albeit split between London and home. On the plus side, I was refreshed and had the resolve to make the required changes.

I then embarked on a quest to reinvent the business, which took two years. I appointed three directors to work with me and invited input from all the staff and, together, we re-imagined the company. During this process we came up with three core, long-term objectives which all carry equal weight – to build on our reputation for excellent client work, to provide a first-class working environment for staff, *and* to make a profit. The only other time I told an audience about the equal weighting thing – they laughed.

I find it appalling that profit is expected to be the number one priority in business. But then everything is so short-term these days. Yet balancing objectives is what it takes to make a business sustainable and fulfilling. Long-term relationships with clients are key to longevity and these require consistency of staffing. Profit is the oil in the engine but it isn't the only reward. Human development – your own, your staff and your clients (not to mention the impact you have on your community) – is gratifying too.

The process of re-creating the business energized everyone in a way I couldn't have anticipated, and from the beginning of this year I have been able to revert to working two days a week. I have no direct responsibilities now, just the luxury of being the 'glue at the top end' and overall business guardian. So, I have metamorphosed yet again and as a result, I am also now working outside the financial sector too, as a mentor (another new beginning), where I can use my experience to help others develop personally and professionally. I love my life, which moves seamlessly between work and play, combining the buzz of London and the peace of the countryside, horses, socialising and solitude.

Why have I told you all this? Because the never-ending change, constant focus on what's working and what isn't, how to be better and the process of re-inventing myself, have been enormous catalysts in my journey to discover the 'ultimate relationship'.

I am going to leave you with 10 business insights I have gained along the way:

1. You can't move an organisation forward unless everyone is singing from the same hymn sheet. Control doesn't work – at least, not for very long. It takes a huge amount of effort and is not self-sustaining. It's far better to create values that can be shared and which attract people to your oganisation; values which create a sense of belonging and add something to everyone's working experience.

2. There is no such thing as the truth (not one version, anyway). Everyone sees the same situation with rose-tinted spectacles

according to their experience, expectations and baggage. The only way to avoid bearing grudges when things go wrong is to try and see it from the other person's perspective – most people are doing the best they can from how they see it. Few are downright malicious.

3. Trust your instinct in order to make better decisions – if you can locate it?! We are trained from an early age to use our intellect, so it is actually quite hard to recognise instinct. Simply put, it's how we feel about something or someone. It's an inner guidance system which defies logic and is much more accurate. So, be prepared to go against advice and convention. When you have learned how instinct feels and have had positive experiences from acting on it, it will start to become your default.

4. Once you have decided on a course of action, fantasise about the outcome. Imagine it, feel it, breath it, smell it and live it in your mind and in your senses, until it's almost real enough to reach out and touch. Then it will be the next logical step in your reality and not such a massive jump, as to be unbelievable. Then and only then, can it happen. Remain open as to how. You don't know what you don't know and, with a little divine intervention, there could be something outside your experience and knowledge which brings it about.

    This is an example – I had a clear idea about the property we should move to (our fifth and most recent move). In my mind it would be quiet, open-plan, a blend of period and modern, with air-conditioning and good neighbours. I was excited about how it would feel. I was living in it in my imagination, prompted by the shortcomings of past premises. Then, out of the blue, a long-lost acquaintance contacted me as a result of seeing me in the media and we had lunch. He mentioned his firm was thinking of buying a building and they would need a tenant. I mentioned we were looking to move. Within a month they had found a building. We moved in within three months of that lunch meeting. It ticked all the boxes, with the added bonus that there was no agent's fee to pay.

5.   Take care of yourself – your physical, mental, emotional and spiritual health. Everything comes from you. Explore what keeps you well, sharp, balanced and inspired. The more in balance you are (ie feeling good) the better it gets. And the better it gets, the better it gets. It's a classic virtuous circle.

6.   Don't make decisions unless you are in that 'feel good' place. This is where you have the strongest connection to your instinct and will make the best decisions, with the least risk of mistakes. Develop a variety of means of getting back into balance if you lapse. Only you can do this. The question is, how long do you allow it to take?

7.   Build an excellent reputation. Reputation is everything; it can make or break you and it takes time to build. It's partly about principles and partly about standards. It means being fair in your business dealings, so consider how you would feel if you were on the receiving end of your actions, whether as a client or customer, staff member or supplier.

      It can be useful to create guiding principles for more difficult interactions. In a talk by Marjorie Scardino, which I attended in the 1990s (when she was probably the only women CEO of a top 100 UK company), she said her guiding principle was 'generosity' and she measured her difficult decisions against this; it also shaped her culture. I have a number of guiding principles which help me when I am unsure of the right balance in a situation. They include truthfulness and honesty; respect for myself and others; integrity in all dealings with all people; wisdom; transparency and gratitude.

8.   Recognise fear and train yourself to overcome it. Fear is the biggest obstacle. Fear of failure, fear of success, fear of being found out, fear of being hurt and fear of anything else you care to think of. Fear can be useful, briefly, when it acts as a warning against danger but when it stops us realising our potential, it doesn't serve us.

I suspect we will never be entirely free from fear as it's part of our human condition. But we can challenge ourselves to overcome it when it creeps up on us, and this will increase our performance no end.

I have worked on this throughout my life in different ways. For instance, I experienced physical fear in sport. Rowing at top level hurts and you know you will have to go through the pain barrier every time you race. In the equestrian sport of eventing where you are galloping to huge fixed jumps, it's scary as there is a high risk of injury if you or your horse makes a mistake. I have also done a few one-off sensationalist things (which I won't be repeating) such as a tandem free-fall jump from an aircraft at 10,000 feet and a tandem sea dive down to 30 metres.

I haven't dealt with my fear as well as I would have liked, it has to be said. I have done what I have done in spite of being afraid, which wastes a lot of energy, though I used visualisation to see myself coming out of each experience safe.

Another form of fear I have experienced is 'stage fright', ie doing interviews on live TV and giving talks to hundreds or, on one occasion, thousands of people. One stand-out TV interview was ITN *Lunchtime News*. I was waiting on the side of the large and intimidating set, watching the programme going out live a few feet away from me, before it was my turn to go on. The subject was not really my specialty. I was prepped as best I could be but my mouth was dry, I felt short of breath and my heart was beating out of my chest. I wished I could spontaneously evaporate!

I found myself wondering why I was so nervous and, in a flash, I realised it was the fear of performing badly and letting myself down, which was ego based and selfish. I quickly flipped my thinking and focused on the fact that I was there to impart useful information to the viewers, who were less knowledgeable than I was. The nerves vanished into thin air just as I was called into position and the interview was a success. This change of perspective has helped me ever since.

We face all sorts of fears every day, especially when running a business. Fear of phoning an important client, fear of criticising the performance of a member of staff, fear of making a colleague redundant, fear of asking the bank for money. My approach in these situations is to get clear on what I want to say, visualise the desired outcome, fake the confidence, open my mouth and let the words fall out. It's OK to 'fake it until you make it'. With practice it gets easier until there is no faking. Here is an expression I have used a lot in these situations, 'If not now, then when?'

9.   Have faith. This is a difficult one. Faith is something most of us only discover when we have our back against the wall . In short, when we are out of options and when logic and reason have failed us. I'm sure many of us will have been in that situation at some point in our lives. For me, ironically, when I have had the courage to let go and had faith that things will work out, a solution has emerged.

Here is another property related example – they tend to have large price tags and be critical decisions, hence super-stressful! In the early years, I moved the business twice in quick succession as we grew. When we needed to move again, I felt we should have somewhere we could stay for at least 3-5 years to justify the cost of moving and to create stability for clients and staff. In truth, we couldn't afford to take on that amount of space as it would cost three times the rent we were paying at the time. But we couldn't afford not to either. I was in an invidious situation. Everyone I spoke to advised me against it. I crunched the numbers and knew we would go bust 6 months after moving if we didn't dramatically increase our revenue. I cried myself to sleep for a week!

All I had left was instinct and, though it was a bit surreal, at some level I felt at peace with the move. So, I took the plunge and launched into the unknown. At the end of 6 months (almost to the day) we gained a substantial new client which gave us the time we needed to grow the business to match the new cost base. At the time, it felt like a miracle. I had walked up to my front door each evening during that six months, wondering how long I would continue to own my property!

It is at times like this I know I'm not alone and that there's a divine helping hand. But we don't have to be in crisis to invoke this help. In small ways, we find examples in everyday life which we call coincidences, such as chance meetings, thinking of someone and they get in touch or stumbling across valuable information which leads to a new opportunity or a solution. When coincidences keep coming and we can't call them random anymore, we see them as synchronicities. Acknowledging this allows us to recognise the invisible support which is always there for us and, in time, it becomes a dependable force and an immensely useful time-saving tool, which appeals enormously to my sense of efficiency.

10. Success is different for everyone. I have learned it's about what makes you happy. Being driven is fine but achievement doesn't make you happy if you are driven straight on to the next thing. You don't have to give up material wealth or creature comforts to be happy. It's about being at peace with yourself and the world around you, and accepting that values, priorities and a sense of balance is a moving feast. So, continual adjustments and re-adjustments are necessary.

In closing then, I have no doubt that the ultimate relationship is the one with yourself. Undoing the illusions I acquired from an early age about me, my family, friends, partners, colleagues and life in general has been profound and is a journey without end. Getting to grips with who I really am has been painful, yet astonishing. It has been an adventure into the unknown, a great gift and each new chapter is a process of discovery and an opportunity to re-invent myself and my world.

Here is a short talk I gave to a Head Girls Conference in 2002. The theme of the conference was leadership. I loved talking to young people before they entered the working world. During the 17 years I ran my women's financial services company, I took 6 placement students from various universities to do a year's work with my firm. I felt responsible for giving them a positive formative experience, as I knew that important choices might be based on this later on. And I loved to see their talents develop during their stay with us.

Passion

How exciting to be standing in front of the next generation of leaders, movers and shakers. Some of you might even make history one day. Perhaps a few of you have a dream, a burning desire, a passion to do a particular thing in life, and that will certainly make it easier because you already know what direction to go in. For the rest of you, it will be down to experimentation, a process of trial and error when you start working, perhaps for the first 10 years or so, which will probably tell you more about what you don't want than what you do. It doesn't matter too much where you start. But it's vital to keep searching for your passion and when you find it, have the courage to follow it. Passion is where you can maximise your talent and shine in the world. When you are in this place, you have the power to make a difference to others.

Why is passion so important? Well, think of the people you admire, the teachers you have learned the most from, the sports coaches who have motivated you. What do they have in common? Passion for their work, and from that passion comes charisma which is infectious and inspiring. They are natural leaders in their fields and generate respect and co-operation without even trying.

People who are passionate are excited about what they do and want to share their enthusiasm. So, there is often an altruistic dimension to it as well. Alternatively, people who are driven by ego and ambition lead by coercion or manipulation in its various forms.

Another characteristic of leadership is instinct, and this is related to passion. Oddly enough, instinct isn't part of our formal education, yet! The academic world values logic and reasoning above all else. Yet the quickest, most effective and most accurate tool for making decisions is instinct. Instinct *first* (which points you in a particular direction) and logic *second* (to work out the detail). We are all born with fully functioning instinct, yet it is trained out of us, and most people live their lives completely disconnected from it. This makes everything much harder. So, we need to rediscover it in order to fulfil our potential.

What does instinct feel like and where in your body do you find it? It's the first reaction you have to a situation and you have to learn to notice it because it's fleeting. It's usually in the solar plexus just under your ribcage, the place where you get butterflies. When you feel tight there, it means 'proceed with caution' and when it feels soft and relaxed, it's 'green for go'.

So how does this connect to passion? Have you noticed that passionate people have an energy around them which you can sense from a distance? They shine when they are talking and seem larger than life and this draws people to them. Well, passion also draws situations to you – the things you need to make your vision a reality. For instance, chance encounters with the right people, vital information, an idea triggered by a conversation. Passion is a heightened state of awareness and it puts you into balance. When you are balanced, you can engage your instinct, which is your internal 'sat-nav'. Passion raises your antenna in a world of infinite possibilities and instinct guides you to the right place, at the right time.

It can be disconcerting though, as instinct usually kicks in at the last minute, like a signpost at a road junction. If you lose faith and become negative (a form of fear), you lose connection with your instinct, so you miss the signpost. Then you think instinct doesn't work, so it becomes disabled.

If you want to be a leader, find your passion. If leadership is not what you want, find your passion anyway because it will change your life and you will be a beacon to those around you. Actually, this is also a form of leadership. And we all know that when we feel good, life is effortless. But when we lose this feeling (which happens to us all from time to time), having passion in our life helps to re-balance us quicker. Life without passion is no life at all, it's merely existence.

I am going to finish with a few words about women's entrepreneurship. This is a phenomenon whose time has come. We have reached a critical mass and are now on the radar, which is a cause for celebration. Increasing numbers of women entrepreneurs across the globe are creating significant economic wealth. Women in poorer nations are doing this too, lifting their communities out of poverty by starting their own micro businesses. In short, millions of women are being liberated by their own enterprise and this brings financial freedom and choices.

Women have a noticeably different business style to men and generally go into business for different reasons. They tend to be more holistic, inclusive, long-term and customer-focused. They value ethics and integrity. Money, status and power are not usually their main objectives and they also set up more social enterprises. Many start their own business to get a better work-life balance, or because they have reached the 'glass ceiling' at work, or to fill a gap in the products and services they need for themselves and their families. They are more risk averse and usually grow their businesses more slowly.

With our ability to listen, our innate sense of teamwork, and sensitivity to the bigger picture, we are playing an increasingly important role in bringing a sense of balance to the business world. And it's only a matter of time before we apply our problem-solving skills to the world beyond business. I look forward to seeing the changes you will bring to this important time in history.

This talk is on how to network. I gave it to senior women at one of the UK's largest management consultancies, in 2001. Networking is an essential business skill but it's the Achilles' Heel for many women. I struggled with the idea initially (it's probably bound up with issues of self-worth). So, I thought about it strategically, to avoid coming away frustrated and empty-handed from a networking event and wasting a valuable opportunity.

How to network

Networking is an art

In the professions, many women don't like the idea of 'selling' their services and I am one of them. It smacks of persuasion – convincing people they need something they don't and implies manipulation, or worse still, intimidation. I would far rather do business with people who want to do business with me, so I prefer the idea of being approached rather than doing the approaching.

I have absolutely no problem with marketing and promotion to let people know what I do. This creates a pool of potentially interested clients and, once they have found me, selling the idea of using my services is easy, because I am totally comfortable with what I do in my area of excellence.

This approach is much less time-consuming (and far more enjoyable) than cold-calling. I never did any cold calling, even at the beginning of my working life, because I found the idea of intruding on people to be an anathema – apart from the fact it is a numbers game and is utterly soul-destroying. Instead, I asked my personal contacts if they knew people who might be interested in what I do and I worked from referrals. Later, my participation in women's networks proved to be a natural source of potential clients.

But there is an art to networking and you need to make it work for you. As with all business projects, first decide on a strategy, then commit to it.

- Work out which networks you want to attend, where and when, close to home or work, in or out of business hours.
- Decide what you want from networking, eg new business, peer-group support, contacts or a combination.
- Is a woman-only group or a mixed group most appropriate?
- Is it more useful to network in your own professional field or outside it?
- Is it better to start a network in your own company for mentoring and profiling?

I chose several professional women's networks in different sectors to mine, where members matched my client profile, and also where I was interested in the subject matter and the events. It's best to attend meetings regularly, as it takes time to get to know people before you gain any business benefit. Here are some suggestions for making the most of each networking opportunity:

- Go prepared. Decide that you are going to make 3 or 4 contacts during the event and put out an intention to meet the right people.
- Arrive early. People are less likely to be locked into conversation groups when it's quiet, so it's easier to walk up and introduce yourself.
- Once the event is in full swing and people are standing around in groups, it's a bit more daunting to intrude. But the worst thing you can do is to procrastinate and hover at the edge of the room. Some people will be bored with their group (but are too polite to move on) and will welcome the distraction of a new person joining them. Remember, you are all there for the same reason, which is to meet new people, so it's legitimate to interrupt conversations. I found this challenging to start with, as it can bring up self-worth issues. For instance, do I have a right to 'barge in' and will people be interested in what I have to say? But you have to take a deep breath and do it anyway. Like all new skills, the more you practise, the easier it gets.
- I usually say, "Do you mind if I join in but please don't let me interrupt your conversation". That way I don't feel as if I am being rude or spoiling anything and I have the advantage of listening for a while before contributing. Gauge if there are likely to be any potential clients in the group but don't be too keen to say what you do. You are bound to be asked before too long and if not, wait for a lull in the conversation, then ask what everyone else does. Someone will ask you in return and, if not, you can offer it.
- If there are no business opportunities, politely withdraw from the group. "It's been lovely meeting you all. I guess, I should do some more networking now." Don't be embarrassed to do that. Maggie Thatcher famously talked about 'working the room'.
- Develop your 'elevator pitch' so you can describe what you do quickly and succinctly. In the early '80s I didn't like saying I was an independent financial adviser because of the reputation the sector had for mis-selling. So I said, "I advise women how to

look after their money." In the service sector, it is often better to describe what you do rather than offer a nebulous job title, which is meaningless to most people.

- If you get on well with someone, ask for their card so you can stay in touch, or follow up the conversation if there is business potential. If the latter, it's best to simply ask the person if they would like you to contact them to arrange a meeting. Write notes on the back of each card to remind you about the person. I don't give my card to everyone I talk to and I don't ask for cards from everyone I meet either. Be selective.

- If you say you are going to follow up after the event, do it promptly, and if it doesn't result in an outcome, leave the ball in the other person's court. You can always invite them to a business event you are holding in the future. If someone is interested in what you do but not in a position to become a client at that point, then ask if you can keep them informed about your services through periodic emails or a newsletter. My golden rule is, 'be polite and professional and don't act in a way that you would find unacceptable yourself'.

- Get into the limelight at networks. Most networks are on the lookout for speakers to include in their calendar of events and favour their own members. Find a good angle on your subject and volunteer. You can also get involved on a committee where your name will appear in communications to members, and you will have a chance to meet other committee members more regularly too. Or volunteer to write an article or a column for the newsletter or magazine.

In my experience, women network in a more subtle way than men, just as they have a different leadership style. It was very much a man's world in the 1980s when I started working. The business stereotype was male and aggressive, not something most women aspire to. But through my participation in networks, I realised that other women in business thought like me, and this was a revelation. It made the idea of leadership much more appealing. Being a good networker is a vital business skill and part of the toolkit of every 'business athlete'.

In 1990, there were only 1300 women Independent Financial Advisers out of a total of some 26,000 in the UK. I decided to set up a network to support them, based on the benefits I had gained from being a member of professional women's networks myself. It was a pioneering time for women in the financial world and the culture was difficult. It was male and patronising and women felt isolated. Here are the talks I gave at several of the network's key events. The first is an extract from the launch event.

Launching a new era

On the leading edge

I bet you've never been to an industry gathering like this before? It's a bit different to the usual events we go to, where we are the lone female. Feel the power in this room. See the talent around you. Remember it and tap into it frequently when you leave.

I have to admit I've been overwhelmed by the response to this initiative. Over 160 of you registered to come tonight and more than 350 have asked to join the Group. Embarrassingly, my target for the first year was just 250; I completely underestimated the appropriateness and timeliness. Your emails have reminded me how challenging it is to be a woman in a man's world. Some feel it more than others but we all are aware of it. One of you said to me, "At best I feel misunderstood, at worst isolated".

It's an interesting place to be, out on the leading edge. Granted, it's uncomfortable but the flipside is that we are pioneers and everything is possible. We can't change others to improve things for ourselves, that's a thankless task and mostly impossible. People deal with their own stuff in their own sweet time. It's much easier to change ourselves – our thoughts, beliefs and actions and, in so doing, change the world around us because how we are, determines what we get.

We attract what we are focused on, whether it's what we want or what we dread. When you are professionally isolated, it helps to be in a slipstream of positive energy to support you in focusing on the right things. And that's what the Women's Independent Financial Adviser Group (fondly known as WIG) is about. WIG will provide peer-group support and encouragement, the buzz of like-minded women and inspiration from women speakers we admire, to help us feel good about ourselves and the work we do, and raise our expectations and our performance.

When I started out as an Independent Financial Adviser in 1983 (my first and only career), I was shocked at the absence of women, especially after university where they were approximately half of the total. I went out looking for a female peer group and joined all the professional women's networks I could find – about half a dozen or so, which were just starting up in London at the time. I owe much to these groups for the support and encouragement they gave me and the wonderful friends I made, not to mention the idea to start my own business focusing on advising women. In the build-up to launching WIG this evening, I have re-experienced these benefits and know that this group has the power to move us all forward.

The network's gala dinner became an annual fixture in the financial calendar for a number of years. It was a big unpaid job that I could only do because I had delegated most of the day-to-day responsibilities in my own business, and the network's monthly events were, by then, run by others. I felt passionate about showcasing what women brought to the profession. The annual awards set out to find the best women advisers in the country and put them under comprehensive and exacting scrutiny. It was a real accolade to win. The awards were reported in the national and the trade press, which elevated the status of the winners and raised the profile of female Independent Financial Advisers (IFAs) to the public. An audience of around 350 at this first gala dinner in 2002 included senior financial men (colleagues and bosses of the women members), who were 'sitting ducks' for what I had to say and, as you would expect, I didn't mince my words.

Feminising the financial world

Championing financial women

This group has astonished me, perhaps it has you too? It seemed little more than a moderately good idea initially. There were too few women advisers in the sector – less than 5%. So, as an advocate of women IFAs, it seemed that the task of addressing this gross imbalance should begin with me. After all, my firm has consisted exclusively of women advisers for the last 15 years, and is especially attuned to the particular strengths and values women bring to the business of being an Independent Financial Adviser.

At the risk of being contentious, it's my view that the sector, run by a male elite, is in a bit of a state and it's high time women began to play a serious role in shaping our future, not just the future of our clients. That's what the Women's Independent Financial Adviser Group (WIG) is about. What does it mean on the ground? Well, for a start, it means supporting and encouraging women IFAs to achieve their potential and be recognised, which is the purpose of these awards. Also, by creating a common voice, our views will be heard and this will enable us to attract more women into a sector that is uniquely suited to them.

Why is it suited?

- Because it's client focused and allows women to use their highly developed listening and relationship-building skills along with their professionalism and integrity, to develop trusting, long term relationships with clients.
- The job is intellectually and emotionally stimulating.
- It requires a high degree of multi-tasking (a skill which is in our genes through eons of child-rearing).
- It offers a flexible environment so women can combine work with their family life, as well.

Unsurprisingly, the culture in which women thrive is not the one most commonly found in the financial sector. We know (through research we commissioned) that the single most important factor for women IFAs is to work in a supportive and nurturing environment. This is a higher priority than money. Money is important but not as important as culture. What's key for women is to be somewhere they can develop personally and professionally. We are long-termers and often start more slowly than men, which boils down to lack of confidence. But this is rectified over time with knowledge and experience and, interestingly, many women advisers become more professionally qualified than their male peers.

Unfortunately, the predominant culture in our sector measures success by short-term performance and leaves many women feeling they have failed before they have even started. This is also a barrier to women entrants. In addition, covert sexism which still flourishes in many organisations is an additional hurdle which can grind even the strongest women down, over time.

If the sector wants more women IFAs (and it desperately needs new blood, as the average age of the majority male financial advisers is 52) then changes must be made. Women will make a unique contribution because of their different approach. What do they bring to the financial world?

- More women in client-facing roles will start to change the tarnished image of the sector. The public will begin to trust financial advisers again and this will be good for everyone. It will also make the choice of a career as an IFA more appealing to women.
- Women are long-term thinkers and strategists, and this will create more sustainable businesses.
- Women's natural leadership style is inclusive, which will get people working together within their organisations and in the sector at large.
- Women are client focused, so they will create more balanced and ethical business models which will help to reinvent the financial world.

In case the men in the audience are worrying, we are not after global domination! We just want to have an influence in and add value to our sector, making it a better place for practitioners and the public alike.

Having envisaged a different future, let's take a quick look at what WIG has achieved so far:

- We have 1200 members, which is the majority of women IFAs in the sector.
- Meetings are run nationally in 9 locations, a total of some 40 events a year.
- All our activities are free to members. WIG is funded entirely by the financial community which means that many leading men in the sector support our aims. Thanks to those of you who are here tonight.
- We have created our own interactive website.
- We have commissioned several pieces of research, most recently into the public perception of male and female advisers. The results are interesting and will be published shortly.
- The annual awards which we are here to celebrate tonight, will promote women advisers in our sector and make them visible to the general public, via the national press.

This is no mean feat. What we have created is special and it provides a means to change our future. It is a great opportunity which is timely and appropriate, and reflects a turning tide.

I ran the annual awards and gala dinner for 4 successive years. It was the highlight of the network's calendar and greatly anticipated by all. It was high profile, glamorous and fun but it was an exhausting single-handed undertaking that had to be squeezed around the edges of everything else in my life. For that reason, it wasn't sustainable. Leaving the sector gave me the exit I needed. I still cherish the happy memories of this special event, as do all the winners, I am sure. In this final talk, I took the opportunity to make a 'call to action' to the financial community.

Grand finale

Final awards event

"The world is round, not flat". What a revelation that must have been! Can you imagine the complete and utter change of perspective that this one discovery brought to people's lives, in an instant?

Though a little less sudden, we are seeing the start of a sea change in the business world which will gather momentum and, ultimately, be no less significant. Women make up 51% of the population and, in time, we will take up our rightful position of power and influence in the professions, business and politics, for no other reason than it is essential to include a female perspective in global economics and the governance of our world.

The 2006 awards tonight are symbolic of this change and recognise the coming of age of women as powerful contributors and decision-makers. We are on the radar, and a mix of economic, social and demographic pressures will increase the momentum of this change. Though the financial sector is lagging behind, we have our own particular catalysts which will, I believe, accelerate a catch-up.

Ironically, some of the current hot topics in leadership training draw on attributes that are traditionally regarded as female. For example, empowerment as opposed to manipulation, or intimidation. In 'academic speak' transactional leadership is the old 'carrot and stick' approach, eg 'if you do 'x', I will give you a gold-plated carrot', hence a transaction. Whereas transformational leadership (the empowering stuff) is about inspiring people through creating a culture of success.

Another hot topic entering the British boardroom is 'emotional intelligence'. Emotions have been seen as a female domain and a weakness in business, up until now. But leading-edge research recognises that the best decisions involve something beyond the intellect (yes, emotion) and that the best leaders have empathy with the people they work and deal with, which is a traditional female trait.

Women are also known to be more cautious investors and also business managers and this affects their leadership style, too. Similarly, women business owners tend to borrow less money than men and grow their businesses more slowly. This long-term approach has great benefits.

These traits, plus a more holistic approach to client management, make women excellent at building trust. So, if they can overcome the cultural impediments to their progress in the financial sector, then in the long term, they frequently become big business producers with outstanding persistency records.

However, to help women advisers reach their potential, we need to recognise their differences and create environments in which they can thrive. Also, more female role models will inspire women in the back office to cross the line into advisory positions, attract female graduates and possibly lure women from other sectors, as well.

Why bother? Well, ignore the 'female factor' at your peril! It's well known that accountancy and law have done better than the financial sector in recruiting women. But while women account for roughly half of new entrants, few reach the higher echelons for all sorts of reasons including blocked promotions (known as the glass ceiling), promotions designed to ensure failure and prove that women are no good (known as the 'glass cliff') and organisational inflexibility making it impossible to combine family and work.

What is astonishing, though, is that the proportion of women entering medicine and veterinary science has utterly changed. Today around 80% of applicants are women, a complete reversal of the not so distant past when 80% were men. This means that even with the inevitable drop-off of women, sheer numbers dictate that as they progress up the ranks over the next 10 to 20 years, some professions will be run almost entirely by women.

In time, we are likely to see a similar scenario elsewhere. So, it makes sense to embrace this development and reap the rewards. In our sector, the majority of men are over the age of 50 and will be retiring in the next 10 years. There is currently no established means of replacing them, either from the graduate market or elsewhere. This could be a catalyst to increase the number of women entrants and help us close the gap with other professions.

As much as a gender shift is inevitable, it is also desirable, because women advisers, with their empowering style, will do a great deal to restore the confidence of a scandal-rocked public.

I came into the sector 23 years ago and I was one of a small handful of women. When I set up my women's IFA business 17 years ago, I felt as if I was right out on the edge. Interestingly, if I was setting up today, it wouldn't be nearly as difficult to raise money because an affluent female market has been proven. There are now more young female millionaires than male millionaires and more female pensioner millionaires than male ones. There are some 360,000 women who have an individual net worth of over £750,000 and many of these would prefer to see a woman adviser.

The media is onto it too. Apart from various female rich lists and lists of women to watch in business, *The Money Programme* recently aired a special edition, called 'Filthy Rich and Female'. So, economically, it would be foolhardy to ignore women clients, who are no longer a niche, or to thwart the progress of the women advisers who are best placed to serve them.

But corporate culture must change in order to optimise these returns. Businesses need to allow women advisers longer to establish themselves and they must stop talking about 'selling'. Women respond much better to values than sales targets, as the latter has connotations of manipulation for personal gain. I will elaborate.

Recently, I was asked to talk at the senior women's network of a multinational management consultancy, which is attracting 50% women entrants. It's the same old story – few women are reaching the top. Usual barriers to success were discussed in the meeting, which was chaired by the company's male CEO, who is supportive of women's development. The biggest inhibitor, as it turned out, was that women dreaded breaking through to the top only to have to meet rigid sales targets.

Women didn't consider themselves to be salespeople and, as such, they didn't believe they had the necessary skills. Yet they were good at all the things which characterised top people in their organisation – they knew their subject, built long-term relationships, gained repeat business, were good at spotting opportunities and worked incredibly hard. I suggested they change their terminology. Simply replace 'sales' with 'business', and swap 'targets' for 'results'. This met with unanimous agreement. It's a start. But words are cheap without the cultural buy-in to support them.

Finally, a thought for the women financial advisers and aspiring advisers in this room tonight. Recognise what you are good at, be passionate about your work, focus on creating excellence and be an example to others. Each of us can make a difference and it's up to us to play our part in bringing about the changes we want.

Article

A year before I sold my women's financial planning business, I was considering what I might do next. I felt sure I would continue to promote and empower working women in some way. So, I was interested to know more about a particular charity I had come across that did just this, albeit in the developing world. This is an article I wrote in 2003 after returning from a field trip to Uganda to see how the charity worked on the ground, assisting the 'poorest of the poor' – namely the country's women. Remarkably, it is courageous women who are pulling their communities out of poverty and assuming local leadership roles, in many developing nations across the globe. It seems to me that this is a microcosm of the macrocosm of emerging female power which is so needed to balance and heal our world. We have much to learn from the world's poorest women.

Empowering the poorest women

The day I arrived in Kampala, capital of Uganda, there was a newspaper in my hotel bedroom sporting the headline, "Kony chops off men's genitals"! Not only did it sink in at the speed of light that I really was in the third world but I became uncomfortably aware that I had arrived in a country at war and known nothing about this. How naive was I? Kony was, by all accounts, a ruthless tyrant and his rebels were running amok in parts of Uganda, for reasons I knew nothing about. A week later, on the day I left, the same paper carried the headline, "All-Share Index launches today". These two headlines sum up the extreme contrasts of Uganda for me.

Much of the land is extremely fertile and green enough to rival the UK, in spite of being on the equator. This is because a substantial part of the country borders Lake Victoria. In addition, there is almost daily rainfall. The people are incredibly industrious and gracious, working from dawn to dusk to earn their daily crust.

Slums run almost into the centre of Kampala, as do the tin shacks and mud roads. This is a society which gives true meaning to the expression, 'Necessity is the mother of invention'. I saw rubber bands holding a printer together in a bank, someone driving a small motorbike with another broken-down motorbike crossways on the saddle behind him and other wondrous sights.

Yet, the poverty is breathtaking. I went to Uganda to visit the slums and their poor inhabitants to find out about the work of Opportunity International (OI), a charity I was getting to know. I recognised a connection with my own business – both are essentially empowering women through financial independence, albeit in totally different cultures and settings.

I saw no tourists, no postcards and there was nothing I wanted to buy in the shops (to my amazement), as all that was on sale were the bare necessities of life – food, clothing and household goods. The stench of rotting meat in the sprawling markets made me want to heave, as there is no refrigeration, so that is how it is sold and eaten. The poorest women are usually married in their teens and have 8-10 children by the age of 30. They endure polygamy and are frequently abandoned by the husbands after having vast families. Even if they are not, many husbands do little to support them and their children. Putting one meal on the table a day is tough and there is negligible running water or electricity. In addition, virtually all education must be paid for privately. The women I met work from 7am to midnight every day of their life, just to exist.

They cook from raw ingredients which includes extracting sugar from sugar cane. They wash their clothes in a bucket, fetch drinking water daily (often miles away), look after their children and have to find ways of earning a living too. They truly are the poorest of the poor. Even so, many speak passable English as this is the business language in Uganda. I quickly observed that the word 'problem' doesn't exist, they use 'challenge' instead. All smile, shake your hand and greet you with, "Hello, how are you, you are most welcome" (to their one room shack). There is no begging or harassment of foreigners.

This charity has been doing astonishing work for 30 years in the developing world, along with other micro-finance organisations which help the poorest of the poor in many countries, to become self-sufficient and improve the quality of their lives. From here, personal and community transformation is possible. This is completely different to charitable hand-outs which last for a nano-second in the scale of things. To quote a much-used phrase, it is about 'hand-ups'. In Uganda, OI work with Ugaforde, the micro-finance organisation on the ground (one of 75 such organisations in that country alone).

Around 85% of those taking loans are women and there is an incredible 98% payback rate. I visited many loan-holders and saw the difference it was making to their lives. They could put two meals a day on the table, were sending more (in some cases all) of their children to school, improving their homes and creating community projects for the good of their family, friends and neighbours.

Western bankers could learn a lot from the micro-finance process which, to me, boiled down to some very basic principles. First, educate before lending. These people have lived hand to mouth all their lives with no concept of borrowing or repayment, or running a business for that matter. Many are illiterate. So, the first step is that they attend 8 obligatory training sessions over as many weeks before they are given a loan.

The first loan equates to around £150. Some buy seed and tools to work the land, others build an extension to their house so they can work from home making crafts, or the loan might fund a shop (ie a small cubicle on the side of the road) to sell their produce. Others buy manufacturing equipment such as an old sewing machine. Basically, micro-loans for micro-businesses. Once repaid, most take out 2-3 bigger loans over the next few years until their business becomes self-sustainable. When the loan cycle stops for one individual the money is lent to another, so it remains in circulation.

After a loan is agreed, the lender supports the borrower in a variety of ways. There is a weekly meeting of each group of loan-holders in their community, with a loan officer, where they discuss business issues and make repayments, along with a small amount of savings, which is obligatory. Failure is not an option as all group members cross-guarantee each other to get over the problem of having no collateral.

The meeting is conducted in a business-like fashion sitting on the grass outside someone's home. There is a self-appointed chairman, secretary and treasurer. Minutes are taken, repayments and savings are logged in a ledger and passed over to the treasurer who banks them. The loan officer frequently uses these meetings to provide additional training on other key subjects such as health issues. Education, support, group commitment and starting small are key ingredients to successfully banking the poor. These are principles which could benefit lending in the West too.

The women I met were a complete inspiration. One group of single mothers each had their own small businesses and had decided to start another one jointly, to ensure they had an income all year round. So, they created a fish farm which was something new to the area. In their non-existent spare time, they spent 3 months digging an area the size and depth of an Olympic swimming pool which is now bearing its first crop of fish. Their ages ranged from 20-75.

To these women, the loans were a lifeline which they grabbed with both hands. As a result of their endeavours, many are now sending a child to university. In fact, I met two women who each had a child doing a Master's degree! The children know their best (and only) way out of poverty is through education and their biggest wish in life is to go to school. Doesn't that put our society to shame?

I was as fascinated by their life experience, as they were by mine. They couldn't understand why someone as 'old' as I was (a very young 43-year-old, in my view) wasn't married, didn't have children and didn't want any. "What on earth do you do with your time?" they asked. Or perhaps I was a prostitute? In turn, I was horrified at them having so many children and having to share their husbands. We all laughed at the absurd, fixed positions of our respective societies.

OI and its partners are passion-driven organisations, or should I say compassion-driven? Actually, they are both. They are rooted in Christianity, so the word God does come up from time to time. However, it's not in your face and they are not missionaries. In fact, if you take the G-word out of it and just use a few of their underlying principles, you'll find some leading-edge practices within their organisation that we can all learn from.

First of all, their faith means they believe it's their calling to serve the poor. It gives them a shared outlook, a commitment to each other and to their clients. My experience of spending time with Ugaforde is that they do what it takes to get the job done, and relish in making a difference to people's lives. They have a vision, mission statements and core values.

Each day begins with a group 'devotion' where psalms are read, followed by a discussion about current happenings in their world. Then hymns are sung (we are talking rhythm, clapping and spontaneous harmony which certainly gets the energy up first thing in the morning). The group closes by deciding who and what might need some 'divine' help and sending prayers to many and varied recipients. These might include children taking final school exams, a client having trouble repaying a loan, a woman who has gone into labour early, treacherous roads in the capital Kampala and so on. They also express gratitude for what they have.

If you don't believe in a divine creative force, then you can call the morning ritual 'coherent group thought' which, in fact, has been shown in science to be real and have an effect on people and events. It's about setting strong intentions for your wants and needs and those of others, along with an unwavering belief that there is a solution to all problems. Expressing gratitude has also been shown to be an important part of well-being.

At a personal level, I have been working on exactly these ideas in my own life for the last few years. After having done things the hard way most of my working life, I have been searching for a way to 'work smarter' (I'm not just talking time-management or delegation). I have found that aligning my thoughts and beliefs before taking action is the quickest way to create more of the outcomes I want.

What do I mean? Firstly, you need to find your passion as this is the engine for 'launching' thought energy. Then make sure your belief system matches what you want, ie that you truly believe you can be it, have it or do it. Belief is about trust in the unknown. This is all we have when the way is unclear, or we find ourselves outside our experience and knowledge. Conversely, when desire and belief is not a match, the result is negativity in one form or another and progress is likely to be erratic.

When you are lined up at an energetic level (you with you), you experience amazing synchronicity guided by your instinct which takes you to where you want to go, often in ways you cannot imagine. It's such fun working this magic and it's what the people of Ugaforde do instinctively, as they tackle challenges in the business of helping the poor.

Before I left, I wrote a poem for Ugaforde which I read at one of the morning gatherings.

To Ugaforde with love

Ugaforde, thank you,
You've been so kind.
I came here to explore,
With very little in mind.
Except to find out what you do
How you work, through and through.

To visit your clients in the field,
Witness their issues
See how they are healed
Through your hard work,
You do not shirk.

I saw your country, lush and green
And it's people with their dream,
To progress in life
Reduce their strife.

To build their country once again
To free their women and then?
To put Uganda back on the map
There'll be no disputing that.

God is with you every day
You listen to what he has to say,
Your belief is strong
Affirmed in song,
The power of prayer
Evidenced everywhere.

Living in the moment
At one with all,
You are magnificent
You stand tall.

Changing lives, giving hope
Other countries, take note.
You've found a way where there was none
Banking the poor
Job well done!

Blogs

My experience 'rewilding' in Wales from 2015 – 2021 marked the polar opposite of 20 years of working in London. I was never really a city person but, for the most part, it was an exciting time. However, once I sold my business, I gradually reverted to my natural habitat which was the countryside.

In moving to Wales, the pendulum swung full tilt in the other direction. With hindsight, I think it was necessary to experience both ends of the spectrum in order to find the balance (which is still a work in progress).

The following blogs are a selection of my writings at the time. They describe the trials and tribulations of living alone on an ancient farmstead in the middle of nowhere, looking after my animals and being the steward of 10 acres of land, positioned in a microclimate of extreme weather. I had three horses and 6 to 8 cats (depending on who was in residence at any time). I was competing in the equestrian sport of endurance which required extreme fitness from me and my horses, managing an internet business and renovating the property inside and out. It was tough. I underestimated just how tough. It took all of me. I had to dig deep, and I found solace in the natural world.

A question of survival

13th January 2017

Today, I so very nearly lost the plot. It was the day from hell, with extremities of Welsh weather, including ice, snowstorms and an arctic hurricane which made it almost impossible to do the horses. Survival was the name of the game. I felt as turbulent as the storm and honestly wondered, more than once, what the hell was I doing rewilding in Wales? For the first time in a long time, I thought it might be too much. Maybe Friday 13th had something to do with it?

Everything was testing – making the yard safe to get the horses out of their stables so I could turn them out briefly (it was a toss-up as to whether they were safer inside or out, given the ridiculous wind which threatened to take the roofs off the buildings); then making the yard safe to bring them back in later; mucking out in a blizzard and the 'icing on the cake' which was the field shelter drama. Unbelievably, the wind had lifted the super-size cast iron shelter over the fence (which it demolished) and placed it on the other side, the correct way up with just a few bits of guttering missing. Repairing the fencing in the hurricane was a challenge and all this made me late getting back to my desk, so I missed an important conference call, which was embarrassing.

However, by dusk, the wind had subsided from crazy (my anemometer registered gusts of 100 mph in the morning) to moderate and when I looked up, I found the sky was smiling at me. The sunset and the glistening snow were stunning. It was the calm after the storm. We (the animals, the buildings and I) had survived and I could breathe again.

Annoyed with myself for losing the plot, I asked the higher, all-knowing aspect of me for an insight into why this had happened. "It's so you know what it's like to be balanced again" came the response in my head. "It makes it clearer what peace feels like so you can find it more easily next time." Good point! My personal blizzard was over.

With supper in the oven, the wood burner lit and the cat snoring by the Rayburn, my re-boot was complete.

Timing is everything

25th February 2017

Changing seasons

Whilst enjoying my daily indulgence of coffee and cake in the garden today, I pondered the glorious scene before me. I live in the middle of nowhere with breathtaking beauty all around and, today, nothing could be heard except the tweeting of birds and bleating of newborn lambs. The countryside isn't always this perfect. Just a week ago,

I was battling horizontal rain, gales and freezing conditions. How quickly things change.

From my garden seat, a large hill, aptly named The Globe, fills my vista and it has just started to turn a shade of spring green whilst the first daffodils of the year have appeared in the garden. The sun was so warm (after a frost first thing) that I was down to just two thermal layers which is almost unheard of, and sporting a peaked cap and sunglasses. Meanwhile, my horse, Talisman, had also ditched his thermals and was wearing a thin summer rug, probably the closest he gets to naked and it's only February!

I don't imagine winter is over yet. While a change in seasons is inevitable, the timing is variable. This premature feeling of spring is the result of a confluence of factors including rain, sun and wind in the last few weeks which led me to muse about the timing of the things we want to create in our life. I have learned from personal experience and also from studying metaphysics, that when you use the power of thought and energise it with feeling, what you want to create becomes a reality in your future and, provided you remain balanced (which allows for connection with your intuition), synchronicity will guide you to it.

But what often happens is that we block the process, by being impatient. We start to doubt it will happen because it hasn't yet and this becomes the dominant vibe we send out to the field of infinite possibilities we are all entangled with. So, our creation doesn't manifest. Worse still, we might manifest what we don't want because the field responds to what we are strongly focused on, whether it's what we want or not. It's the physics of frequency. If, however, we learn to notice when negativity creeps in and distract ourselves, or find other ways to stay balanced and patient, then what we want and have created in our future *must* happen – it's only a question of when.

Timing is crucial and is subject to change because other people who might be part of a synchronistic chain of events that leads to our manifestation (just as we are part of theirs), can change their minds or become negative and drop out of the chain. Or, other people with a stronger focus might enter it. This is a multi-dimensional phenomenon which I am sure will be explained by science in the future, especially as entanglement, the field and the effect of thought are already established fields of research.

Meantime, absolute belief in the power of thought to manifest things is vital. You have to 'know it' with certainty in order to create it – just like when you place an order in a restaurant and know, without doubt, that your meal will arrive. But unlike ordering a meal, it pays to be open-minded as to how your creation will be delivered and exactly what form it will take, because it might be even better than you imagined! After all, we don't know what we don't know.

Secret lives

8th December 2017

Hedgehog matriarch, a resident on my yard

Serious snow made life challenging with the horses again today. The conditions changed minute by minute, from brilliant sunshine to white-outs and back again. How extraordinary, beautiful and cruel nature is!

Late last night before the white stuff arrived, whilst it was blowing a gale and painfully cold, another extraordinary event took place. I was in Talisman's stable tucking him up before I went to bed when I heard a strange noise on the yard. We all heard it, the cats, the horses and me and all of us stood there motionless trying to work it out. Then 'it' emerged into view under the yard light.

I had recently made the acquaintance of a little person who, unbeknown to me, secretly lives under the floorboards in the ancient barn. There are steps up to the wooden door (which has a cat-flap fitted for small feline friends) and the steps are large and uneven, so it's a bit of a challenge if you are a small furry creature carrying something heavy.

I have met him twice. The first time, I just got a glimpse of his bottom as he disappeared down through the gap in the floorboards to his lair, when I entered the barn. The second time, I heard a rustling in the hay when I was preparing horse feeds in the barn. I peered over to investigate and, there he was, just a couple of feet away. We eyeballed each other for quite a long time, both thinking "What on earth are you doing in *my* barn?!" Then I had a little chat with him before he scampered off about his business.

His face was so cute but I didn't know what he was, so I got on the computer and looked up all manner of species until I saw him peering out of the screen at me. A polecat! After more investigation it turns out they are a protected species, having been on the verge of extinction, but are starting to make a comeback in a few parts of the British Isles including Wales. How lucky am I? So, I now have resident horses, cats, hedgehogs *and* a polecat and those are just the animals I know about. I am going to get an infra-red camera to film the nightlife and find out who else lives here, as there are frequently holes in my woodchip tracks, in the muckheap and, sometimes, in the fields too and it would be good to know who the perpetrators are, as well as what they are up to.

So, back to last night. As we all stood peering into the dark, the little fellow was using all his might to drag something larger than himself under the gate and down the yard towards the steps of the barn, where he came into view under the light. He saw me and briefly stopped to acknowledge my presence before attempting to summit the mighty steps. He dragged the 'thing' up the first two steps towards the cat flap and then got stuck. The 'thing' occupied the whole of the second step and he just couldn't get the right angle from the step above to exert enough leverage to heave it up, or from the step below to push it. Up and down the steps he went, tenaciously considering his options and trying to complete his mission, before admitting defeat.

All the while, we (the audience) held our breath and watched in amazement. Then he turned and stared at me and I knew he was asking for help. So, I went across the yard, picked up his catch by its legs (which turned out to be a bird of prey – how on earth did he manage that?) and pushed it through the cat flap. Yuck! I retreated quickly, hoping I hadn't frightened him off and that he would return for his catch.

A little later, I went back to check and was delighted to find the bird had vanished. The polecat had dragged it down through the floorboards but its feet were sticking out as it was too big for the hole. Not wanting the cats to rob him of his hard-earned supper, I found a broom handle and pushed it as far as I could under the floor. I could still just about see it but a few minutes later it had vanished completely, so mission accomplished for the polecat – with a little help from his friends.

I was gobsmacked and utterly thrilled. I love the fact that there are secret lives on my yard and even more, that there was tangible communication between me and the little wild creature who was so trusting. Yet again, how extraordinary is nature?!

The path to freedom

7th March 2018

The swirling blizzard continued relentlessly day and night and whipped the heavy snowfall up into drifts of 10 to 15 feet in some areas around the house, yard and fields. Bizarrely, other areas had almost no snow at all. It was surreal.

The drive looked like a frozen sea, with huge waves coming over the hedge leaving the horse-walker and turn-out arena barely visible. Snow found its way into every building underneath the doors, through joins between the walls, gaps in the roofs and every other nook and cranny. Nothing escaped.

The stables on both sides of the yard had snowdrifts inside them. Talisman was covered in snow each morning. Fortunately, he couldn't feel a thing under four layers of rugs! Poor Elizabeth (the yard cat) had a blanket of snow on top of her as she slept in her bed in the barn. It was useless sweeping it out of the buildings as it blew straight back in so, reluctantly, I gave up. It got me thinking how nature has the power to completely obliterate all evidence of life.

Digging paths with a shovel had to be done several times a day, in order to get the horses out of their stables in the morning into a large shed they could socialise in, then back into their own stables at night. There was absolutely no other option for them, they were well and truly grounded. In fairness, they coped really well. Talisman couldn't believe his luck that the horse walker was out of bounds and that he was off ridden duties too.

Feeding the feral cats in the barn up the drive was challenging and required a 'Scott of the Antarctic' impression from me. The drive was impassable, so I took a shovel and dug steps, one at a time, up the bank in the field to get to the barn. I was up to my thighs in snow but the girls were pleased to see me, so the daily expedition was worthwhile.

Unfortunately, during this whole testing episode, I endured a lot of pain with a raw toe, the result of a chilblain from a previous cold spell. So, I have been hobbling and this was the hardest part of it all. It also added a degree of hazard to certain domestic tasks. Balancing on one leg whilst hoovering, for example, resulted in a classic own goal. The hoover pipe got suctioned onto the rug in front of the wood burning stove and as I pulled it away, I lost my balance, tipped backwards and 'smack', the pipe hit the stove door with such force that it shattered the glass.

It might have been funny in normal circumstances but I was gutted. It's the room I live in and the stove is on every day. Bryngwyn (ever present feline house companion, yard manager and personal trainer) and I are now marooned in the tiny kitchen, huddled around the Rayburn, until the wood burner is fixed. And I have no idea when that will be as I am cut off.

Another incident I could have done without during this Arctic period, was the rotting corpse of something hairy under the floorboards in my bedroom. The smell was utterly vile and it meant sleeping with the window open (yes, in minus 12). The endless joys of country living!

Today, I decided I had better check my remaining food rations. I figured there was enough to last until the weekend but as the drive was still covered in massive snow drifts (despite recent rain and rising temperatures which have started the big thaw), I decided to phone a neighbouring farmer to see if he could pick up some provisions for me when he was next in town. However, he was busy lambing – ironic considering the weather!

Whilst pondering another plan an hour or so later, I heard a rumbling outside. I ran out to investigate and to my utter amazement, I was greeted by the farmer on his tractor. He had taken a break from lambing to dig me out. I was overjoyed to see him and thrilled to set eyes on 'the path to freedom'. Extreme weather is a catalyst for creating community, and my community just came to rescue me. As it turns out, I was the last in the area to be reconnected with the rest of the world. Thank you, thank you!

So, for now, I am euphoric. We (me and the furry entourage) survived the worst of conditions. I kept my composure (mostly) in the belief that I am safe and that my instinct will nudge me when I need to act, ensuring I have enough fuel, food and horse essentials, do repairs to buildings ahead of dire weather and have back-up plans for all eventualities (plus a few). And that I will be in the right place at the right time, if things go pear-shaped.

My growing connection with nature and the elements is part of this. I am increasingly attuned to the weather and have a feeling for what's coming (as do many who live on the land). I also have confidence from having dealt with many and varied crises in life, that somehow, I will come out smiling.

I apply the same principle to the world at large. Despite what seems, I see the world heading in a new direction through an evolving global consciousness which recognises that, fundamentally, most of us want the same things in life, which are safety, health, peace, prosperity and happiness. I see disasters and systems failures leading to massive innovation and new beginnings in ways we can't imagine. Of course, the when and how remains a mystery. But expectation of good outcomes is a powerful catalyst and I look on with excitement about where we are headed.

What my animals have told me

28th April 2018

Bryngwyn - a blend of other dearly beloveds!

Did you know you can bring your beloved animals back to you when they pass on? This is my experience, several times over in fact, and they don't necessarily return as the same species. I found my current house cat Bryngwyn at a local cat rescue centre. Despite vowing never to have a long-haired cat again, he caught my eye because his markings were virtually identical to a cat I had loved and lost a couple of years previously. I was speechless when I saw him as it could have been her.

I also lost a much beloved Jack Russell terrier shortly after the cat (both were elderly when they went and had been best buddies). Then, a little later, I lost a special horse. Three in the space of a few years. Their names were Panzy, Benjamin and Norris respectively. It turns out, all three have returned to me wrapped up in the furry little feline Bryngwyn, who is the love of my life, along with my Arabian 'princeling' Talisman, his pal. He has all three of their personalities and characteristics down to a tee. And Norris had the characteristics of another special horse I'd loved and lost before him. I used to feel sad that our wonderful animals had such short lives compared to ours but I now know they can be with us forever, if we want them to.

Something else I have discovered over many years of having an animal family, is that they have much more sophisticated means of communication than the limited vocabulary of whinnies, meows and woofs we attribute to them. Whilst it is recognised that body language is a powerful training tool because animals use it in their own social groups, I have also found they are masters of telepathy, so we can use this to communicate with them too. Most people who have cats and dogs will have had some experience of this, for example, arriving home to find your beloved pet waiting for you.

The way I use telepathy to communicate with my animals is to say their name (several times) to get their attention and then talk to them while I simultaneously project a visual image of what I am saying. The picture should be as if the animal is looking out of their own eyes. I have used this in so many different ways but here is one example. Horses often get stressed when they see their 'limo' on the yard and realise they are going somewhere. Much projectile pooing usually follows! So, I began to show my horses a picture of what they were going to do when they arrived at the destination, or a picture of where they were going if they had been there before. A big sigh usually followed, and they calmed down. This is a fun technique to experiment with on your animals.

On a slightly different subject, we are not the only ones with past lives, it seems. I have had numerous 'past life readings' on my horses and cats from a variety of people who have the gift of being able to communicate with animals. Generally, I use an animal communicator when I have drawn a blank on a particular behavioural or health issue and need information directly from the horse's mouth, so to speak. Often, this brings up previous lives I have had with my horses. But in all cases, it has provided answers and was a beautiful, moving experience which was healing.

Our animals frequently have wise messages for us too. The experience of hearing what they have to say has put a completely different perspective on animal consciousness and intelligence for me, as well as how to train them, as they don't think in the linear way we do. They tend to cluster similar experiences together in their memory.

I would like to share with you a few of the messages my animals have given me over the years. The first horse I had in my adult life went off his food at a certain time every year. He wouldn't eat his twice daily feed rations and dropped weight. It was at the change from autumn to winter. He told the horse communicator that the grass loses its sweetness at this time and is bland. So, if his stable food was also bland he wasn't inclined to eat it. But he could be encouraged to do so, if something sweet was added. A little molasses was duly included in his daily rations and he licked the bowl clean. Simple!

On another occasion, I had a horse that was always 'in your face' and not in a good way. He would nip and bump me and interact in any way he could; if I was on the yard and he was in the stable, he would bang the door, shake his head, whinny and generally create a fuss every time he saw me. It became very annoying.

He told the horse communicator he had been a war horse in one of the great French battles. His soldier was shot and slumped over his back barely conscious and they wandered away from the battlefield. The horse was exhausted and stumbled into a ditch. He was stuck and couldn't get out. After the battle, he and the soldier were found and the soldier was pulled out of the ditch. Normally, if a horse couldn't be rescued, it was shot but for some reason, he wasn't. He kept calling for help to no avail and eventually drowned in the rainwater which filled the ditch up. The emotional hangover in this lifetime was the constant cry for attention, through any form of interaction possible. Knowing that, helped enormously as I could understand him rather than get cross, and the problem lessened over time.

Another example was provided by my cat Panzy. When a psychic friend came to stay, Panzy made her presence known (continually), which was unusual. My friend thought she had something to say and indeed she had. In fact, at that time, Panzy was called Fanny (short for Myfanwy). She told us that domestic animals have 'house names' – the ones we call them but they also have 'proper' names. Her name (and I quote) was *"Panzola the third, like my mother and my grandmother before her"*. Henceforth, I changed her name to Panzy and she bestowed upon me much more affection and attention which was a great honour, given she was of such esteemed bloodlines!

Counting my blessings

16th May 2018

Al fresco dining

'Walking your talk' is one of the hardest things to do in life. Talking is the easy bit – thinking, living and being 'it' consistently, is much more difficult. So, when a large number of extremely irritating small issues recently threatened to rock my equilibrium (wreck it, to be more accurate), and I ended up grumpy and lacking in humour with the animals, I decided it was time to re-group. I have a variety of methods I use to regain my balance but, on this occasion I found myself 'counting my blessings' and it was a long list indeed.

Biggest on the list on that beautiful summer's day, was the fact I could eat every meal 'al fresco' whilst admiring a world-class view from my garden seat and observing the wildlife. Gratitude! I flashed back to contrast with 20 years in London building a business when I rarely saw the light of day, boiled in summer in old-fashioned offices, froze in winter, held my breath to cross the polluted roads, commuted several hours every day, and where the enduring theme in life was challenge and change.

I thought how wonderful it was that I finally had the freedom to live each day as I choose, with no responsibility to anyone except me and my animals. One thought led to another until I was feeling my usual perky self again. I had pulled back from the brink of the slippery slope, where things can go pear-shaped very quickly.

Conflicted

1st June 2018

Harmony at home

I live happily at both ends of the spectrum. Expansive, extrovert and centre-stage is how I lived during the first 20 years of my career. Building a business from scratch took that and more. It was full on, day and night, and the never-ending challenges provided never-ending opportunities to learn. The type of business hadn't been done before and the sector I found myself in was alien to me, but I thrived on breaking new ground and making it up as I went along.

It was tough and stressful though, for the most part, I loved it. During this time, my only let-up was visiting my horse at the weekend and my parallel spiritual journey which helped me to sustain peak performance with few holidays and minimal sleep. It also gave me a perspective on the crazy world that was my life.

All that said, my home has always been my sanctuary and wherever I have lived, whether owning or renting, I have endeavoured to make it beautiful and soothing to the soul. And that's the rub. The draw of my home has always been a source of conflict, as I am equally happy being a recluse, which has been my life for the past 10 years – a gradual process of simplification eventually led me to the polar opposite experience of rewilding in Wales. During this time, I stopped consuming the media, didn't socialise or see many people. It's been just me, the animals and the natural world, plus an internet business and competing in the sport of equestrian endurance.

Once again though, I have reached a pivotal point. I feel a need to get out and engage with the world again, so another adjustment is pending. And that's the thing. Nothing stays the same for very long. We need to make continual adjustments to regain our balance, or we atrophy. I just hope the next one will be less dramatic than the last. But I'm not banking on that!

Only I can fix me

5th August 2018

Animals are great healers

With the weather remaining hot, the ground is scorched and the grass has stopped growing so, incredibly, I have been struggling to find enough grazing for two horses on 10 acres! The only upside is that I haven't had to spend endless hours on the tractor topping the normally lush pasture, which has freed up time for other things such as being a bit more sociable, and this included having a house guest.

A special friend came for a few days' refuge. She found herself in a dark place over the last few years, with many issues, health and otherwise, running on empty and surviving on willpower alone. I am pleased to report that she went home smiling (and eating)! I can officially say she bounced off the bottom and has begun the steady climb out of the abyss back to health, happiness and realising her enormous talent which will be a gift to mankind one day, I am sure. But it got me thinking.

It's so easy to lose your mojo as life pulls and pushes you every which way on a daily basis. In fact, the moments of equilibrium are generally the exception rather than the rule, for most of us. And once things start to go wrong, life can escalate out of control in the blink of an eye.

Regaining equilibrium is an art form (maybe one day it will be taught in schools). But we have to know what it feels like in order to find it. For me, it is a feeling of being energised, positive, powerful, believing the world is a great place, seeing good in people and situations and having enough energy left over for others. By another name, this is happiness.

Anything else, is a feeling of being off-balance where our focus is on the opposite which, of course, is all things negative. And negativity, whether anger, frustration, resentment, depression or apathy, is rooted in fear. When we are off-balance, we feel it in our body too, through tension, palpitations, poor sleep etc.

It was an epiphany moment when I realised that no-one and nothing could fix me, but me. Whatever tips us off-balance, it's our choice as to how long we wallow in unhappiness and prolong the pain. The quicker we recognise the clues and practise techniques for restoring our vibe, the quicker we get our life back!

Don't ask, don't get!

18th August 2018

On the house front, there's been more decorating – this time the rear sitting room which is the most spectacular room of the house and certainly worthy of a lick of paint. It isn't my favourite job (not even close) and, as usual, I completely underestimated how much work was involved until I started taping up two recessed doors, a recessed window, a fireplace recess and a ceiling full of beams, nightmare!

Hours of using a small brush to paint around all the edges was required before I could get the roller out. Finally, there was a large radiator to paint. The nearest I have got to an intimate relationship for quite some time was caressing the radiator, to coax a first coat of paint to stick to the shiny surface. It has since been pointed out that I could have sanded it to get greater adhesion. But as I was a 'decorating virgin' until recently, I don't have many tricks of the trade yet. Live and learn.

I did stop for a minute, though, to admire the perfectly preserved, exquisite wood panelling on a section of the wall, which really is a piece of art. And then an idea popped into my head – I would 'commune' with the ancient wood which must be nearly half a millennium old. Energetically, it would hold the wisdom of nature even though it was long since felled to serve the noble purpose of supporting my house.

I haven't lost the plot. I believe we are connected to all things through our consciousness, as everything (including us) is ultimately energy and 'tree huggers' are a known species of man (and woman) who can feel the energy of trees and receive their wisdom. Even though I wouldn't count tree hugging amongst my hobbies, it wasn't too big a stretch to think that the wood panelling might have a message for me. I did feel a little silly talking to the woodwork in my sitting room, I have to admit. But I popped the question and, to my surprise, a thought dropped straight into my mind. Whether it was from the wood, or maybe the wood inspired me to dig deep into my own wisdom, I don't know. But this is what I got:

"If you stand in your magnificence, which is your birthright and that of all mankind, you will be noticed (as I am). Therein lies the potential to touch people and change lives."

I was gob-smacked. Definitely a case of don't ask, don't get!

A love-hate relationship with the news

27th September 2018

For the last 15 years, I have abstained from a daily intake of mainstream news and disposed of my TV. The only connection with the world beyond my own life was a magazine called *The Week* – a 40-minute read which summarises global news from the previous 7 days, plus a lot more. This, of course, meant I was always out of date when a major crisis hit, or if there was a high-profile death like the Princess of Wales. My ignorance provided much amusement for my family and friends.

It wasn't always like that. For the first 20 years of my professional life, I was an avid consumer of news, including the financial media, as I worked in that sector. But I became disillusioned with the unrelenting menu of negativity, drama and hysteria which had become the stock in trade of journalism and the mainstream. This was coupled by the rise of celebrity journalists whose opinions, often based on scant credentials, claimed more column inches than the experts and who bullied and berated their interviewees on TV and radio, to score points and inflate their already oversized egos.

Meanwhile, the politicians and senior figures they interviewed were opaque to the point of uselessness. The whole thing was exasperating, depressing, lacking in respect and utterly devoid of integrity. It seemed to me that the media had lost its credibility and was perilously out of control.

There was also constant repetition which I found patronising in the extreme, ie telling us a key story was going to break, such as an important report or a government announcement and, not only that, telling us what would be in it! Then telling us when it actually happened and telling us again later. At worst, it felt like brainwashing and, at best, space-filling. If the latter, why not include uplifting stories about the courage of those who had lived through catastrophies and rebuilt their lives, or inspiring ideas about re-shaping our world, or life-changing inventions and grass-roots solutions to global problems, all of which go largely unreported. Who says that good news won't sell papers or drive web traffic? I am sure it would do both. People need hope, which also improves health and well-being.

For that reason, I also subscribed to a quarterly newspaper called *Positive News*, in order to get a fix of the good stuff, and started delving into the wonderful library of videos on TED.com. In short, I took control of the news I consumed.

I have always been extremely positive about the world we live in. I grew up at a time when a number of world leaders could have put their finger on the nuclear button and started a war which, almost certainly, would have led to the destruction of humanity and probably the planet – an Armageddon that was prophesied by many ancient sources. I didn't believe for a minute that would happen. I always felt that, despite massive evidence to the contrary, we were on a path to creating a better world and that the prophesies meant the end of an era, not the end of mankind.

The tipping point for me was in the late '80s, when it looked like we were teetering on the edge of the precipice. But a 'wild card' event that nobody had predicted, namely the fall of the Berlin Wall, ended the Cold War and changed the fate of humanity.

A fundamental part of my own outlook is that 'we don't know what we don't know', so anything is possible. Conversely, if we expect the future to be based on what we *do* know ie what's happened in the past, that's exactly what we will re-recreate. So, back to my decision to abstain from mainstream news. Basically, I chose to withdraw from unnecessary external negativity and focus on the task at hand, which was business. This was challenging in the extreme and it took everything I had – mind, body and soul. Staying balanced and mentally sharp for the duration was hard enough without the media 'drag factor'.

More recently, however, it seems the tide is turning – just a little. The mainstream occasionally carries positive stories on its internet sites (though they are not easy to find) and a global movement towards 'balanced' reporting is gathering pace, albeit under the radar. There is also the emergence of a new online news sector made up of independent and alternative platforms, which are focused on unearthing the truth behind the mainstream narratives and providing a vital understanding of what's really happening in our world. Horrifying and fascinating in equal measure! However, you have to look to find them.

Once again, I find myself interested in the news and it seems a good time to gain a broader perspective, as it will help me make informed decisions about my own pending metamorphosis. Being informed also means I can offer long-distance 'energy' support to those affected by crises of one form or another around the globe, and this is something I can do anonymously from my living room, simply by being balanced and using the power of thought. It even has a name. It's been called 'compassionate action'.

Our true human nature

26th October 2018

I gawped in amazement at yet another stunning sunset and was filled with wonderment at how every one is unique and exquisite. One of the only advantages of the short winter days, is that I am outside feeding the horses at sundown and can enjoy the natural 'wall-to-wall art' which is omnipresent where I live.

As I stood there, the thought came to me that, just like nature, we have the potential to change ourselves moment by moment, moving through a kaleidoscope of infinite variety in our nature and our being. We are magnificent just like the sunset but, mostly, we have no idea of our magnificence because our thoughts, beliefs and actions, as well as the people and events around us, tell us otherwise.

That night, as if to reinforce the point, there was a full moon. I was mesmerised by its brightness and perfection from the window seat in my bedroom – nature's very own late-night movie show. It prompted another thought on the same theme. As the moon progresses through its cycle, we see just parts of it. But it's still whole.

Most of the time, we show only part of who we really are – the rest is obscured by the 'clouds' of life. But, on the rare occasions when we shine our light fully and we are all that we can be, we too are wondrous, radiant and mesmerising, and have a powerful and positive influence on the world.

The challenge is to be this way for more of the time, which goes against the grain of what is considered to be 'normal' human nature. However, as part of the evolution in consciousness that is beckoning, I suspect it's time to re-think the very essence of what it is to be normal.

What makes us who we are?

2nd November 2018

I have always been interested in how the heady mix of our human 'make-up' (early life experiences, family, culture, hereditary talents, spiritual outlook etc) leads us to be passionate about certain things and often guides our path through life. This fascination with human behaviour led me to study psychology. I later realised that the same dynamic also played a significant part in my professional life, especially growing a business to a staff of 35, where people proved to be the critical factor time and again. Today, when I watch movies, I generally choose ones about real people and their life stories, for exactly this reason.

As it happens, I recently watched a film called *The Fifth Estate* about Wikileaks and its founder Julian Assange. In many ways, Assange was a 'wild card'. He had a strange and disturbing childhood and became an unusual man, driven by his quest for exposing corruption. He was flawed (as we all are), admired and despised in equal measure. I could see how early influences and Assange's psyche played straight into his profound mission to cast a light on so much that is obscured in our world. It cost him dear, as we all know.

The film laid out the sheer scale of corruption and deceit in all corners of the 'legitimate' world, from business to banking and government. Despite a smear campaign to irrevocably damage Assange, he and his collaborators were forerunners in setting the scene for the growing culture of 'whistle-blowing' today. Perhaps, in future, it will be possible to expose corruption without retribution?

Or maybe, whistleblowing will become redundant as more people find the courage to speak out and reveal truths which are impossible to ignore, demonise or squash. Then, 'the system', largely captured by vested interests which obstructs justice and accountability, could be circumnavigated? Dysfunctional institutions might even evolve into something that works in the interests of all of us.

But going back to the idea of how we are inspired to live our lives. I believe we have many lives and choose the type of human expression we come into each time – not necessarily the details but the broad potential for experience that will enhance the wisdom of our soul and touch people around us. The important word here is 'potential'. I don't believe our lives are pre-ordained. I believe it's our choice as to whether we fulfil any pre-planned potential or not.

Through many lives, over eons of time, we are able to experience the good, the bad and the ugly, the insignificant and the significant, the happy and the sad, the wise and the ignorant. How magnificent is our soul for doing this because there is so much pain involved. And for those who have a treasure trove of spiritual wisdom (whether they know it or not), what an incredible time it is to be alive right now, with the potential to reinvent ourselves and our world through compassion, integrity and love. This is what's required to work the seemingly unsolvable puzzles of our times and evolve into an enlightened humanity. That's my view and I am inspired by it!

Silencing fear

7th November 2018

A friend has been experiencing neighbour difficulties. She was harassed and it got to the point where she was reluctant to leave her house, felt physically sick when she saw the neighbour and she was contemplating moving. This resonated with me as I have encountered 'neighbour stress' in the past on several occasions and it's unpleasant. Like my friend, the first time it happened to me, the mere sight of the neighbour was enough to give me palpitations and the issue became all-consuming when I was at home and spoilt the enjoyment of my long-awaited dream property.

Even after the verbal exchanges ceased, the neighbour would still send me unpleasant faxes. I felt violated as they spewed out of the machine into the heart of my home, without my consent. And the mere sight of him continued to evoke a panic response in me. Having turned my life upside down to move to this property and invested everything I had in its renovation, the building of equestrian facilities and getting 20 acres ship-shape for the horses, there was a lot at stake.

I was in the middle of nowhere, except for two neighbours, one on either side of me. Basically, a hamlet of three cottages. This concerned me when I bought the property. However, I convinced myself that the upside was I wouldn't be completely isolated. I contemplated moving to get away from the problem, but decided against it, as I hadn't found a way to neutralise the anxiety and I was worried it might become a repeating pattern in the future.

The big question was, how to deal with something so invasive and so personal? After much introspection, I realised I needed to acknowledge the fact that I had a right to be there. If I couldn't do that, how could I expect anyone else to? It would also help me exude an air of self-assurance and confidence that might change the dynamics of the situation. After all, I understood the power of thought and its effect on the people around me.

However, anxiety is rooted in fear and while this exercise worked to a point, it wasn't enough to completely change my vibe. So, I came up with a 'visualisation strategy', which was familiar territory, as I had used visualisation successfully in sport. In the case of the neighbour, I imagined him as a cartoon character whenever I saw him, which made me chuckle. In time, it disarmed the fear and I was finally able to neutralise my anxiety.

As if by magic, the 'intimidation by fax' campaign stopped. Anxiety is a strong negative emotion. My neighbour picked up on it and responded to it. The psychologist in me thinks that, subconsciously, he felt powerful knowing that he had prompted my fear. So, he continued to use my fear against me. But as soon as I changed my vibe, there was nothing to respond to and the whole thing stopped. Amazing!

I have since discovered another ingredient in this type of scenario. Many years ago, I bought a painting from a London gallery. It's the only time I have bought an original piece of art. I found it spellbinding. It's called *Namaste*. I didn't know what this meant. I just loved the painting. Years later, the concept of 'Namaste' has become an important part of my life. It means, "The God in me greets the God in you", a greeting used by millions of people on the planet, though, sadly, not in the Western world.

What does it do for neighbour relations? It means recognising that there is a spark of divinity (the creative source, God, call it what you will) in all of us, and this connects us. Obviously, we have the choice to acknowledge it or not, and use it in our lives. For my part, I am endeavouring to recognise it in everyone, even if they cause me grief. It's a work in progress and it's challenging but not impossible. Don't get me wrong, if I have to defend myself or my property, I will. But I now know that I can only be in control of a situation when I act without fear.

A matter of life and death

11th November 2018

Feral family

This week, an old horse who has been acting as a companion to my horse Talisman for the last few months, is being put to sleep. He's reached the ripe old age of 36 and is now quite disorientated. He also has poor eyesight and has gone off his food, so it doesn't seem fair to put him through the discomfort of another winter. A decision was reached with his 80-year-old owner that this was the best thing to do.

When the vet comes later this week, it's possible that one of my feral cats might also have to be put to sleep. I have become very fond of Lomax (who has moved me to tears on more than one occasion recently). As with the 7 other feral cats in residence, I had to trap this magnificent black feline, so I could get him neutered.

This was a year ago. When I returned home with him, he did a runner. I can't blame him after the trauma of being taken from the wild, into a car, into a town and into a vet's surgery full of strange people and smells, as well as other animals in distress. Anyway, he reappeared three months ago in a dreadful state, though I was touched he had come back to a place he knew was safe.

At first, I thought he had been attacked by something bigger than him. He hid in the barn and just appeared from the shadows to be fed. He was talkative but in a distressed sort of way. I took pictures for the vet, who thought he might have an extreme allergic reaction and she gave me medication to put in his food.

After more research, however, it seemed he might have ringworm. By this time, I was able to make a fuss of him when he came to feed and, wearing gloves, apply lotions and potions to his sores. Of course, I then had to disinfectant the whole barn and try to keep the other cats away, as ringworm is highly contagious to animals and humans – if that's what he had. We are still in this routine and I am his sole companion. He spends the whole day and night sitting or sleeping on the highest rafters in the ancient barn to keep himself safe, as he's obviously feeling vulnerable.

Ringworm usually goes away on its own after three to four months and we have now reached this point. He improved a little for a while but has deteriorated again and is a sorry sight, with sores from head to tail. So, obviously, something else is going on which is extremely serious. He is struggling to get down from the rafters as he is so weak and he isn't as talkative as before. What a brave little chap he is, especially to trust me to help him. I love this cat and feel so sorry for him. The vet is going to look at him when she comes to put the old horse to sleep – if I can trap him. It's vital she sees him but, at the same time, I don't want to cause him even more stress.

All this got me thinking about the cycle of life and death. A large proportion of the world's population, especially on the Indian subcontinent, believes in reincarnation without any shadow of a doubt. It's fundamental to their lives and to their religions. The situation is, of course, very different in the West where it's a minority view, though one which has always made perfect sense to me.

Musing on this theme, I observed the wonderful autumn colours glistening in the sun (brown, yellow, gold, copper and traces of green) whilst enjoying my daily fix of coffee and cake in the garden. In the foreground was the pear tree, now stripped of life and bare to the bone (or bark, to be more accurate). An irony occurred to me. People love the autumn colours, yet they represent death. Life vanishes once the autumn leaves fall, and the remaining scene is stark. But we enjoy the beauty of this death and accept it in the happy knowledge that, next year, a new expression of life will emerge.

This is a good analogy for reincarnation. For me, the soul is constant and we should celebrate the passing of the human form and the wisdom that has been accrued during a lifetime. If the soul is indeed eternal then death is not finite, it's just an opportunity to re-invent ourselves. While the silence is deafening and the loss overwhelming when we lose someone precious, we can at least gain consolation from the idea that it's not the end. I believe a part of those we have loved and lost lives on inside us.

And as for our animals, that's another story for another blog.

Mirror, mirror?

7th January 2019

What do you see when you look in the mirror? This is a question I have asked myself for some time. For most of my life, I just saw a face – first thing in the morning looking sleep deprived; or in business mode with make-up on looking surprisingly glam; a bit 'feral' when rewilding in Wales; laid bare, no disguises last thing at night. What did I say to that face? Occasionally, "Looking good Fi". But mostly, a big sigh!

Yet the old adage, *'The eyes are the gateway to the soul'* alludes to so much more and I am pleased to say that I can now see much, much more. For a start, I know that physically I am only looking at the outer wrapper of the current expression of my soul. Beyond that, I see a woman with a broader perspective gained from many difficult lessons learned in this lifetime and others. I also see the 'wiser me' who has healed the 'wounded me' many times.

The eyes in the mirror reflect back to me a cellular intelligence that knows how to heal my body and slow the ageing process. They connect me to my spiritual 'entourage' (invisible support group) and to Mother Earth, my biological parent, who is in a conscious symbiotic relationship with us. The eyes remind me of my star heritage and my cosmic family. They tell me that we are all connected energetically in a 'quantum soup' and that the divine spark that lives in me, lives in all of us. This is what I see in the mirror now and I honour the divinity and grand design of it all.

What do I say to those eyes? Congratulations for allowing an expanded consciousness. Congratulations for discovering that though I am small, I am powerful and can change my life and the world around me. Congratulations for realising that my whole purpose is to be the best I can and help others to know that all is well in their world, in spite of what might seem.

A peculiar type of logic

24th January 2019

Bryngwn and his feral 'wife' Elizabeth

Observing my cat Bryngwyn, got me thinking. My ever present 'assistant' was supervising me mucking out the horses' stables, in between adding to the mess by burying his pooh in the bedding, which frequently ends up on the bottom of my boot. On finding himself thirsty, he went to great lengths to drink from the few remaining drops of water in a very large stable bucket, in preference to drinking from strategically placed 'easy-access' cat water on the yard. In fairness, he usually goes for the cat water but, on this occasion, he preferred to do the splits on the edge of the stable bucket in order to quench his thirst. What sort of peculiar logic was this? In JFK's immortal words (which I approximate) "We choose to go to the moon not because it is easy but because it's hard". Obviously, Bryngwyn was thinking along similar lines.

As I finished my horse duties, I found myself musing about this thing called 'logic' and its bedfellow 'intellect' which are so valued in our culture, in education and training and which dominate the way we lead our lives. And yet, this paradigm is flawed. Don't get me wrong, intellect and logic are very useful. It's just that they shouldn't take the lead in our decision-making in every situation.

It's taken a long time for me to re-discover the value of instinct and to use it as the prime determinant in making decisions, which has led to far better outcomes. Instinct is something we are born with and in the very early years of life it's the force that drives us. But education suppresses it because it trains the intellect-logic duo instead. Instinct is still there but it's buried.

Ironically, instinct is our best guidance in life because it gives us the heads-up as to where we can find information and opportunities that lead us to the things we want. Otherwise, we are confined by the box of our experience and knowledge. So, the order of work should be: instinct first (for direction) and logic second (to work out the detail).

At times, we are aware of a fleeting instinct that evaporates before we have had time to properly examine it. We are usually busy doing a task which absorbs us and we only remember our instinct with hindsight, probably after choosing a different course of action that didn't turn out so well.

So how do we reconnect with instinct and how do we hear it above the noise of life? Unsurprisingly, we have to train ourselves to do this. And just as with any new skill, practice makes perfect until a new habit is created which no longer requires effort. But first, we have to discover what instinct feels like and where it resides in our body and our consciousness. This is tricky because it's subtle and, of course, different for all of us.

For many of the smaller day-to-day decisions for the animals and me, such as diet, dietary supplements and exercise, I use a shortcut and dowse with a pendulum. This is my instinct on the end of a piece of string which has the advantage that I can see it. It may sound a bit 'far out' but based on 30 years of experience using it, I have learned to trust it and it has saved a lot of guesswork, time and money.

The importance of instinct cannot be overestimated. I would like to think that, one day, when our education system is more enlightened, it will teach 'life skills' including how to use instinct and, in so doing, better equip children for the challenges that inevitably lie ahead of them.

The reincarnation of Lomax

5th July 2019

The most amazing thing has happened. Lomax is back! You may recall I told you previously about a feral cat I loved, who became ill. I nursed him until the end and, through my tears on the last day, I asked him to come back to me. I had had this experience previously with other animals (large and small) and was confident he would return. But I wondered what form he would take, as I knew he could come back as any animal.

For the record, all the feral cats here are named after previous occupants of my ancient Welsh homestead and, according to the title deeds, a certain Lord Lomax was once in residence. Lomax 1 (who passed away) was jet black, in contrast to the other ferals who are all white and something. Lomax was a very handsome fellow. But in the shadows of the barn where he lived, he was mostly visible by his beautiful bright eyes. So, whatever animal he came back as, I knew I would recognise those eyes.

A few months after he died, I saw a flash of black on the yard out of the corner of my eye and wondered if it was the 'spirit' of Lomax. However, a few days later, I came out in the morning to find a real-life beautiful black cat sitting at the yard gate, waiting for me. He even let me get close and talk to him, which was amazing. The connection was immediate (as it had been with Lomax 1) and he listened intently, doing that 'squinty-blinky-love' thing with his eyes that cats do.

This was a totally feral cat who was not only identical to Lomax 1 (I really hadn't expected that) but trusted me enough to allow me to come within a few feet of him. Remarkably, he was also at ease with the other cats, who didn't scream at him or chase him away. In fact, they sauntered over to greet him, as if he were a long-lost friend. This has never happened before. When a new cat moves in, there are stand-offs and scuffles for a few months until the new arrival establishes a hunting territory and somewhere to sleep, which is acceptable to the others. This was indeed the case with Lomax 1.

A few days later, I found Lomax 2 sleeping on the seat of the tractor in the garage, which had been a favourite place of Lomax 1. So, I have now created a 'feeding station' in the garage for him and he comes to call when 'room service' arrives. The other cats respect his food and stand back and let him eat – again, completely unusual. I am hoping I will be able to touch him soon. The whole thing is utterly extraordinary.

I probably shouldn't be surprised, as my first beloved cat Panzy, who passed away at the grand old age of 19, morphed into my current house cat Bryngwyn, who not only has her personality and mannerisms but also her looks right down to the brown blodge on his nose. What joy and comfort it is to know that our beloved animals can return to us.

It's all in the mind

16th July 2019

I take my safety seriously, especially when travelling. It's not a lottery. I am responsible for me. I have had my fair share of accidents in the past – in cars, on horses and in a variety of other situations, which have prompted a radically different way of thinking and behaving.

For instance, when I was studying in London and in the early days of working there, I was attacked twice. Once out running and the other time on a tube train. I was lucky to escape unharmed on both occasions although, obviously, I was shaken. At the time, the big lesson was to take all practical measures to protect myself such as avoiding public transport late at night, only running in well-lit, safe areas of London, crossing the street to avoid anyone or anything that looked suspicious and, at all times, exuding confidence in my body language.

Accidents on and around horses later on, resulted in injuries, some of which had long-term consequences such as several concussions, an amputated finger, ripped cartilage, torn muscles and ligaments. The takeaway from those situations was to be fully focused at all times with horses, so that I was aware of any changes in their behaviour (usually lightning quick) which spelled danger. Being focused also made me more aware of environmental dangers. If I had niggling doubts about anything, then I took note and adapted what I was doing to put safety first at all times, even if it took longer.

I also wrote off a couple of cars. On one occasion, I ended up hanging from my seatbelt upside down (the result of skidding on black ice on a country lane). On another occasion, the sportscar I was driving spun 180 degrees after aquaplaning on a dual carriageway. It went airborne, flew off the road (in between juggernauts) and landed nose downwards in a nearby ditch. Oddly enough, in both situations, I felt a weird sense of calm as the accident played out in slow motion. And on both occasions, I got out and walked away without a scratch. I wasn't even in shock as, by this stage, something fundamental had changed inside me.

I had started to consciously use the power of thought in all manner of situations, including for my protection. Before each journey, I imagined my car surrounded by a brilliant light which extended in front of me as I drove, creating a safe space. I had learned that thought is energy and, as such, it has a cause-and-effect relationship with what's around me. So, if I invoked an intention for safety then that's what I would get. Divine intervention and intuitive synchronicity would deliver it, even if I was in an accident.

Later, I fine-tuned this idea by adding the notion of 'perfect timing'. Perfect timing also implies safe arrival. So, I expected to be guided intuitively to travel on the right day at the right time, arriving safely and in perfect time. I used yet another version of this when I got on a horse, imaging returning home safely with a big smile on my face.

One by-product whilst driving, was an end to 'road rage', for me, at least. Most of us have an occasional near-miss, often, as a result of someone else's dangerous driving, which raises the heart rate and leaves you incandescent with rage. However, by intending to have a safe journey, expletives such as 'F – wit' followed by aggressive horn-honking, became a thing of the past. They have been replaced by a calm "Thank you for saving me" which I direct to a 'divine helping hand', because I am in charge of me and not a victim of chance and I know that synchronicity will keep me safe.

This type of re-framing is useful in many situations. I was prompted to think about it again recently when giving a mentoring session to a rider who had found herself in a dangerous situation, when riding her horse on the road. They both emerged unscathed but, afterwards, she re-played the 'tape' over and over in her mind, imagining all the dreadful things that could have happened. As a result, her confidence plummeted and she couldn't bring herself to ride out from her property any more. By re-framing the experience to one of thankfulness for being unharmed and explaining how she could create an intention for safety before getting on her horse, progress was made. So much in life is a mind game!

The power of the feminine

10th August 2019

I have been re-reading a number of personal workbooks recently (notes, ideas, issues, insights, epiphanies and affirmations) that I created from around 1990 to 2005. This was during the first part of my career (which was in London) when 'survival' was the name of the game on a daily basis. The reason for this trip down memory lane is that I am planning to write a book, so I thought a quick recap might be useful. In fact, it turned out to be anything but quick, as the 'workbook period' was so intensive. I had forgotten what life was like then, primarily because I aim to 'process on the go' ie understand experiences, integrate the learning and move on, carrying only the pithy essence with me. Consequently, the workbooks were well-used and bulging at the seams.

I was shocked at the sheer scale of my efforts to manage myself and navigate the issues of life during that time. So, it was no surprise that one of the main realisations was that the 'ultimate relationship is the one with yourself'. The workbooks addressed the issues and insights associated with launching various businesses and the challenges they presented, including daily ups and downs, financial crises, people dramas and understanding the part I played in situations, for better or worse. Also, managing my health and vitality, understanding my animals and optimising my fitness and competition performance.

There were also poems I had written, talks I gave and a never-ending stream of affirmations to re-frame my view of myself, so I could create new ways of thinking and being. From my student days when I studied psychology, my efforts to understand myself and my life launched me on a spiritual journey in search of the most profound reasons for everything, through all available means. This included astrology and psychic readings, too. During this time, I worked on my ability to heal myself, honed my instinct as 'guidance mechanism of choice' and explored the bigger questions in life.

As I revisited this treasure trove, one of the themes I noticed was 'The power of the feminine'. I didn't have a positive early experience of this and grew up thinking that to be feminine was to be 'weak', something I resolved I would never be. After stumbling into the financial world in the early '80s, which was male to the extreme (and not in a good way), I found myself setting up a business to create financial independence for women, as I believed this was one of the keys to women's empowerment.

I noticed that I used a lot of male energy to build the business initially, partly because it was the way of the world at that time but also because it came easily to me. I had also observed when I was young, that to be masculine was to be 'strong'. While I didn't realise it, the negative expression of both sexes had had an impact on my early business life.

Interestingly, my business centred on values which I later came to realise were feminine. People and culture took preference to profits, openness and honesty were implicit and creativity was key. I also set up a non-profit organisation to champion the role of women working in the financial sector and a video website which published interviews with top businesswomen, both of which demonstrated women's unique leadership style.

At a personal level, I realised that intuition was the most effective way to make decisions. I also learned that compassion worked better than confrontation. Intuition and compassion are, in fact, two of the things that define the power of the feminine. They are hard-wired into us through our capacity to have and raise children, whether or not we choose to be mothers in the biological sense. These attributes can be used in all walks of life as it is the 'mother' in us that nurtures people and situations. In recognising this, I finally saw the power of the feminine in all its glory and could open myself up to using it and being it.

I am not alone. There is a palpable momentum towards embracing the power of the feminine in so many areas of life. It isn't simply about equality. It's not just about women either. It's about men and women both being able to express female attributes in leadership.

This isn't another box to tick. It is a necessity that will allow us to re-build our flailing world into one which is balanced and equitable.

Personal sacred space

21st October 2019

My home is my sanctuary

The last 6 weeks have been my worst nightmare on the domestic front. Having major work done in the house whilst I am still living in it, is something I vowed I would never do again after a 2-year renovation project at a previous property. How quickly we forget discomfort! In fairness, it wasn't meant to take this long, or be this messy but that's part and parcel of renovating an old property – you don't know what you are going to find until you get going. Usually, it's bad news which adds to the cost, time and mess. But occasionally, there are happy discoveries, though they generally have the same consequences.

This phase of the house project was to upgrade the dark and dingy bathroom and the bedroom next to it, as well as improving the light-less, character-less upstairs corridor created by a previous occupant, to give separate entrances to the bedrooms – the house is 16th century, after all.

Plumbing was tricky when it came to replacing the shower, which meant 'the great outdoors' was the only toilet for me during the day, whatever the weather, and it was brutal most of the time. 'Pissing in the wind' took on a completely new meaning! Some days too, the shower and bath were out of use, so a strip-wash at the kitchen sink had to suffice and given I work outside much of the time with the horses and on the land, that wasn't ideal.

The walls and ceilings in the work zone were covered with distasteful textured wallpaper, which had to go. This was stuck onto thick cardboard which hid the original wattle and daub. The paper was challenging to remove and it was even more challenging to plaster the boards. Elsewhere, there was a lot of filling and sanding to do. And the new state-of-the-art lighting turned out to be faulty and had to be replaced.

Finally, ugly boxing on the corners of the corridor was removed. This was complicated. Under the boxing was some long-forgotten original woodwork which obviously wasn't to the taste of my predecessors, who covered it up. I chose to restore it. However, this meant removing several layers of paint from the wood and blasting off woodworm damage. The walls adjoining the wood then needed repairing. I hadn't fully appreciated the process in advance, as my builder told me it was a "straightforward job". To him maybe, but not to me.

Cleaning up every day was time-consuming (the hoover moaned and so did I) and having to put boots on to go from my bedroom to the loo at night whilst half asleep, was no joke, especially as it involved a trip through 'Siberia' with all the windows open to minimise the smell of glue, sealer, paint and plaster. Try as I may to keep my living area downstairs clean, the relentless banging going on upstairs meant pieces of plaster fell out of the ceiling along the edges of the beams and some of the new grouting in the recently renovated kitchen leapt off the walls. The mess spread and the snagging list grew. In addition, my builder was working part-time to fit in other jobs and was often around in the evenings and on weekends, so there was no let-up. Everything was testing.

My home space has always been a retreat from the madness of my world, especially business. It is my sanctuary and allows me to rejuvenate. It felt utterly trashed. I have no problem getting down and dirty, I do it outside every day but I like the dirt to stay outside. Plus, the constant noise and disruption, lack of bathroom facilities, not being able to have a relaxing bath and a pootle around last thing at night, or be able to get to anything I needed from my bedroom during the day, as well as the constant cleaning, really knocked me off my perch. I got tense, stressed and was spinning in perpetual motion trying to get all my daily jobs done (inside and out), as well as painting the downstairs. There was nowhere to pause and rest for a moment.

I know at some level, that I should be able to live in a state of 'zen' whatever is happening around me but, clearly, I am not there (yet)! It made me realise just how important it is to have a personal space, no matter how small, which is sacred to you – where you can be with yourself, even if just for a few moments here and there.

I am pleased to report that my house is now restored, as is my vibe!

The end?

18th December 2019

The end of a decade is always significant and, invariably, a time of renewed optimism as the new decade dawns. This time, it feels different. Everywhere you look there's chaos – politically, economically, socially, environmentally and every which way. One scandal follows another in the mainstream media, exposing the dark side of life more than ever before. How and what the media reports can have a very destabilising effect on society which makes it difficult to see where we go from here and how we turn things around. Not surprisingly, there is much despair and growing protest. But chaos breeds fear and fear perpetuates the status quo, which suits those who have the most power and influence. This is because a dysfunctional world makes it easier to manipulate people and situations for financial gain and control.

Typically, we use the past as a guide to the future but, for me, that's not a good formula as it usually creates a repeat of unsatisfactory outcomes. On the flip-side, positive solutions are hard to imagine as 'we don't know what we don't know' but it also means that anything is possible, and I like that idea.

Social media, on the other hand, can turn a local crisis into global news in real time, so we all know what's happening in the world. This is a good thing. I think it also makes us increasingly aware that whatever culture or religion we are, our humanity is the common denominator. Most of us want the same basic things in life – peace, safety, health, happiness and abundance; this is a unifying force for good.

But social media also allows us to select information that reinforces our own views, which makes the world a smaller place. And like mainstream media, those who wield the most power (including the platform itself) can feed us manipulative narratives or censor alternative viewpoints.

Amidst the mayhem in our world, there are many amazing things happening – mind-blowing innovations in science, education, politics, energy, housing, the environment and health, which offer great hope for the future. However, to see this broader perspective, we must take responsibility for the information we consume and actively seek out truth and balance. This will allow us to see more clearly and make better decisions.

I am for solutions, not fear. Fear is negative energy and it's dark. Darkness is the absence of light. But when you strike a match in a dark place, ie someone shines their light for others to see, darkness recedes. It's physics. And we can leverage this principle to our advantage. It doesn't take much light to obliterate a whole lot of darkness.

Science has discovered what some of us have known for a long time, that thought has energy. We are entangled in a quantum field that connects us all, and when there is coherent group thought, we amplify each other and are powerful indeed (science also know this).

Dysfunction is systemic in our world and it has been for a very long time, albeit hiding under the radar. Sometimes, it takes an unexpected and shocking event to reveal a bigger picture and this acts as a catalyst for change. Otherwise, left to our own devices, change isn't something we usually volunteer for. This is where humanity is right now. And it's good news. I suspect it will be a bumpy ride for a while but it's exciting to be alive at such an important time – not just the start of a decade but the start of a new era.

Who am I?

28th January 2020

Contemplation

I mentioned that I have been reviewing some old writings recently, which included insights and epiphanies that helped me to deal with the challenges I faced during a fast-moving period of my life. I thought I might write a book about them (this book as it turns out). But maybe my interest in the past was also a little to do with approaching a big birthday. Whilst 'age' is not an institution I subscribe to (as I plan to live to an unconventionally old age, in mint condition), I am aware that I am entering a new chapter of my life.

Since parting with my last business a couple of years ago and simultaneously deciding not to continue competing in the sport of equestrian endurance, I have felt increasingly isolated. I've been reclusive for a number of years whilst rewilding in Wales, though it hasn't been a problem until now. A sense of isolation only crept in after letting go of the 'glue' that gave me a reason to deal with the challenges of such a remote and rustic lifestyle.

On the plus side, the last two years have provided a space for introspection. But it's not been easy or restful, and it hasn't been a productive time in terms of contributing to the wider world either, which doesn't sit well with me. The result was diminishing self-worth, which begged the question, "Who am I?"

In part, the answer came from reviewing these old writings, as I could see that I am the sum of all my experiences, and I am certainly not done yet. Far from it. I can also see that I have earned my stripes. So, I am pleased to say my self-worth is now restored.

In my scribblings, there were a few quotes from books I had read, which particularly resonated with this recent experience. The first is from *Conversations with God*:

Every act is an act of self-definition. Everything you think, say and do declares 'this is who I am'. The question is 'is this who I choose to be?'

My take is that our thoughts create beliefs which influence what we say and do. Not only that, thought is powerful and acts as our point of attraction in the field of potentials that exists all around us. What we think about our self (good or bad) brings us experiences and situations that reinforce this view. So, if we want to change who we are, we have to notice what we think about ourselves. Obviously, this is easier said than done. But with awareness and practice, it's possible to create new thoughts which are more dominant. As our awareness expands, every moment becomes an opportunity to re-define ourselves.

The second quote is from Abraham, a source of spiritual wisdom channelled by Esther Hicks:

You can't be joyful about where you are and not get to where you want to be. You can't get to where you want to be and be frustrated about where you are.

This is a continuation of the first quote. The field of potentials doesn't differentiate between reality and imagination, or between what we feel good or bad about. It simply responds to the physics of energy. The balanced and positive energy of joy is a powerful force for attracting what we want, and the negative and unbalanced energy of frustration is a powerful force for attracting more of what we don't want. Again, awareness of what we think and feel is crucial.

Many years ago, ideas like these required a huge leap of faith for me. I questioned myself all the time, until I had amassed sufficient personal evidence to know that, beyond a shadow of a doubt, this is how things work and you can leverage the system to your advantage. Today, it's different. We know that thought has energy which affects us and our world. Also, as increasing numbers of people search for more in their lives, it's not such a stretch to embrace these concepts.

Identity lost and found

20th February 2020

More rustic me

I spent many years building the brand of my London business, which was really an extension of my persona, as the business carried my name. We (my business and I) were one in terms of image and very much joined at the hip. My spiritual awareness was also visible in my business, but it was compartmentalised then. Me and 'the other me'.

Now, it's different. The spiritual me and my personality are more aligned and the latter feels less predominant. Of course, I am still idiosyncratically me but a toned down, quieter version where the personality is no longer the most visible part. What is more relevant is the meld of the two, and to practise living in 'the meld' as much as possible.

Initially, I was resistant to releasing my personality from its pre-eminent position, something that had defined me for so long (both privately and publicly) and which felt comfortable and familiar. I felt lost. But gradually, I realised the opposite was true. I had found myself.

I have come to understand that our physical being (and all that is associated with it) is a small fraction of a much bigger version of who we really are. It's the essential means through which we express our individuality and our humanity. But, more than that, it's the vehicle we use to experience a meld with our multi-dimensional spiritual self. For me, that is where the real adventure begins.

A moment in time

21ˢᵗ March 2020

I am not going to refer to *'it'* by its name as that feels like energising *it*, making *it* more powerful, giving *it* too much respect. I will just call *it* 'Big V'. In fact, I would rather not talk about it at all but as it's centre stage on the planet right now and the omnipresent conversation, I cannot avoid it. However, I will do my best to offer something constructive.

As real as the suffering is for those who have it, as inhumane as it is for people dying alone because of the perceived risk of infecting their nearest and dearest, and as excessive as the fear-based reaction is (especially from the media), this crisis has the scope to change humanity forever and for the better. The whole scenario is much, much bigger than 'Big V'.

Of course, there will be unsettling repercussions and turbulence all over the world, for some time to come. But on the flip-side, there are a few positives to consider. Will enforced time at home remind us about what's important in life? Will helping those in need engender a lasting spirit of community? Will work become more flexible? Will people take more responsibility for their health through food, lifestyle and the choices they make? Will future education include personal skills that support our physical and mental health? Will powerful and detrimental vested interests in our world become visible so that we can eliminate them? I am upbeat, as always, about the future. 'Big V' is unwittingly uniting us. We are beginning to realise that irrespective of colour, creed or nationality, our humanity is what we have in common.

Because there is so much fear in the here and now, though, it's all the more important to find peace and balance as best we can and to be discerning about the decisions we make. We also have to take things a day at a time, as planning is out of the question in such a state of flux. For those who know how to be balanced, there is a responsibility to be so because it's infectious and the best way to disarm fear in others. It's also a key to health because emotional balance creates cellular balance which boosts immunity.

The world may look like carnage right now but we must remember it's just a moment in time. Profound change is always preceded by disruption, whether personal or global, which galvanises us into a new direction. Once the turbulence is over, change will come about through a quest to ensure that this sort of thing never happens again.

So, my friends, find courage, take heart and be the best you can, as this is far more contagious than 'Big V'.

Many lifetimes in one

28th April 2020

For a long time, I have felt that time is speeding up, certainly since the early '80s. Initially, I thought it was due to a growing connectivity through technology. Email had only just been invented when I started working, the internet was basic, most businesses didn't have a website, mobile phones were new and the few business people who had one needed large muscles (or a trolley) to carry them around due to their size and weight. I was the proud owner of another new gadget, a fax machine.

Fast forward to the present day and it's clear that technology has made the world smaller and more connected because of real-time news and communications. We are much more aware of global issues and the things that are broken in our world. Technology has increased personal productivity too, which adds to the sense of quickening. We pay the price in news overload though, and the absence of any gaps that once existed between things which gave us a moment to reflect, know our feelings and remember who we are. I suspect this speeding up of time is real, not just perceived, and may be part of a larger paradigm shift that, eventually, will expand the limited dimensions of our known 'reality'.

On this note, I believe in the idea of multiple lifetimes, along with most of humanity (more so in the East). I don't think lifetimes are linear either – that's just our construct for the 3D world we live in. More likely, they are in an 'eternal now' where past, present and future are somehow fused and the life we are living in linearity is just the focal point, the tip of the iceberg. Obviously, it's impossible to know for sure, or to get our head around the idea of how it might work, because this is 'other dimensional' stuff.

I believe there is a stash of wisdom we can access from our other lives through the vortex of this one, which we can pull to us to help us solve problems and navigate challenges, individually and collectively. We just have to ask the highest (multi-dimensional) aspect of ourselves to find a way to communicate to the part of us that's in physical expression. This could happen in a variety of ways, including dreams, insights and information.

So, what would it look like if we applied the idea of reincarnation to the speeding up of time? It would certainly be efficient if we could 'reincarnate' whilst still living and save some 20 years of growing up before we can exert an influence on the world. I believe this is possible.

I think it has already happened to me on two previous occasions. Each time, I changed so much I could hardly recognise the person I used to be. The first time was after leaving the financial world and the second was during my rewilding experience in Wales.

The first time, I remember thinking, *'If I could be a totally new person, what would I be like?'* I wrote it down and worked on manifesting the new version of me. The process was more intuitive the next time – I just felt the metamorphosis happening and the outer layer dropping away to reveal the new me. Both times were challenging as it's easy to slip back into the old version of you. But the results were liberating. I have since found I am not alone in having had this type of experience.

I also believe we have much more control over our health and our ageing process than is commonly understood. The secret is to give instructions to our cellular structure. This is a multi-dimensional process. As I understand it, the functionality for this (and more) resides in the 90% of our DNA that is referred to as 'junk'. How could something as brilliant as our biological structure (surely, the highest 'technology' on the planet) have non-functioning parts? I don't buy that story.

So, if we can live longer and access the wisdom of other lifetimes, maybe it is possible to reincarnate whilst still living, by intentionally creating a new version of ourselves. This would accelerate time even further and be extremely useful in our rapidly changing world.

Podcasts

10 years on from the 'Biz-Chat' pieces and several businesses later, I set about describing my experiences rewilding in Wales. In addition to blogs which narrated the semi-feral lifestyle, I wanted to elaborate on my blend of practical spirituality and a quantum version of psychology I had been experimenting with. This arose from the trials and tribulations of life, and a search for solutions to be better and act smarter. So, I recorded a series of podcasts which bring together many of the recurring themes in this book. Mastery of these themes is never-ending, but it provides an opportunity for continuous learning and personal growth. Frankly, life would be dull without that.

The power of thought

8th May 2018

I know this to be true. I have proved it to myself beyond a shadow of a doubt. Because thought has energy, it affects us and the world around us. Coincidences are an example. You might think of someone and the next thing you know, you bump into them or they get in touch. Or, perhaps, you need information and it magically appears. Over time, these seeming coincidences grow and you begin to think that something else is happening, some sort of divine intervention or inspired synchronicity. You wonder how it works and if it can be put to good use.

The first step is to gratefully acknowledge each event and create an intention to experience more of them. The second step is to learn how to work the system, so you can leverage the results. Like anything you want to be good at, it takes belief and practice. There are lots of ways to practise and you will need to experiment to find out what works for you, but here is a small example of something that worked for me and was fun. On long car journeys, I would create an intention to see number plates that bore my initials, or a combination of initials and parts of my date of birth. And just like that, they started to appear.

Gradually, I saw them on all car journeys, long and short, whether I asked for them or not, and so frequently that it couldn't possibly be chance. Obviously, I wasn't looking for them all the time but whenever I did, there they were. Each time this happened, I acknowledged the synchronicity and when a really pertinent combination appeared, I let out a great big 'yesss'. It's impossible to comprehend the feat of organisation, at some level, for all those people to take a journey at precisely the time they did, so that I would see their number plates. What an incredible system and for such a trivial use of synchronicity – which was just to prove to myself it existed and that I could consciously manifest it through my thought.

I discovered further evidence of the power of thought through healing injuries I incurred from time to time. Just bangs, bruises and cuts to start with, using visualisation to stop the bleeding, reduce the swelling, knit the wound and heal more quickly. Later, I amputated a finger. Without recounting the gory details, suffice to say that I was able to clot the blood in minutes and anaesthetise the pain. The finger was reunited with my hand and it healed perfectly in record time. Not a feat I wish to repeat! There's a long list of other injuries I have similarly healed, including several concussions, ripped cartilage, torn ligaments etc. Unfortunately, I have had rather a lot of practice.

Looking back, I think I had an imperative to take matters into my own hands, as it wasn't possible to press the pause button on my crazy life. I was competing in sport and also had the animals, land and a business to look after. So, developing the art of self-healing was extremely useful. I am not exceptional. We all have the same equipment. We can perform our own miracles if we believe we can and commit to learning how.

These experiences made me realise that we must be careful what we think, whether it's about ourself and our health, or about others, or what we expect in life, as our thoughts have the power to deliver what we are focused on, whether it's what we want or not. I have also discovered that we can use focused thought to send love and support to family or friends in distress, or to catastrophic world events, thus making a difference to people and situations far away. The possibilities are endless.

Narrating your life

18th May 2018

Contrary to popular opinion, you haven't lost the plot if you talk to yourself and become the narrator of your own life. In fact, it's extremely beneficial. Most importantly, it helps us to become aware of what we habitually think and do. Only then do we realise how much negativity we carry around and the drama and recurring experiences it creates. To a large extent, we are what we think.

Normally, the most powerful influences in our life are what other people have told us about who we are, or what we can or can't be, have or do. Frequently, this isn't the truth and it's generally not a recipe for happiness either, but it becomes our default programming. In order to change it, we have to begin to notice how our current reality is framed.

This is where 'narrating your life' comes in. It makes our thoughts much more visible and allows us to see how they influence our behaviour. When we are conscious of our thoughts, we can challenge them and if we don't like them, we can change them. Thought, belief, behaviour is the order of things, which is why we must re-frame our self-image and our outlook, in order to create changes that stick.

Changing our ingrained habits of thinking and behaving isn't easy. I know, I have been working on it for as long as I can remember (and still am). But we have to start somewhere, then practise relentlessly, even if there is an element of 'fake it until you make it', initially, because the 'new you' has to outsmart the 'old you' which won't give up without a fight. Practice is the effort required to become more of who you want to be. Others will notice the change in you and it might be a catalyst for them to make changes in their lives too, as we are all mirrors for each other. Some people may drop out of your life because you don't feed their narratives anymore.

It's an evolving process and refinements are never-ending. Our reactions to people and situations provide constant feedback as to what we might want to tweak, which leaves me in no doubt that the ultimate relationship is the one with yourself. Discovering the most authentic version of you is the gateway to self-esteem and balance. It brings everything into sharper focus and becomes a virtuous circle.

Here are some simple exercises you can use to practise the art of narration:

- Choose a practical situation in your day, perhaps one where you are multi-tasking. From a place outside of yourself (as if you are watching you), become your own personal time-manager and direct proceedings for maximum efficiency ie instruct yourself regarding the best order of work in order to accomplish the task. This will help to develop a narration awareness.
- Become your own mentor by providing an internal narrative on situations as they arise. This will provide clarity about what you think and feel and flag up any elements of unwanted programming.
- Next, deal with the 'smelly stuff'! When the 'sh-t' hits the fan, it sets us back. But you get better at noticing when you're at risk of losing the plot as your narration skills grow. The question then is, how long do you take to turn yourself around? A minute, an hour, a day, a week or longer? In time, you won't sink nearly as far with each setback because you will be aware of how things are unfolding and realise when you are perilously close to the edge of the cliff, so you can pull back and avoid plunging into the abyss.
- Lastly and probably the hardest, is narrating what you think about yourself in your daily life. It's usually buried deep but clues can be found in dealing with challenge, conflict and change. All of these take us out of our comfort zone and cause us to question ourselves. The contrast in life is where the real information lies.

Training your instinct

21ˢᵗ May 2018

Instinct is something we are born with and, in the very early years of life, it's the prime force that motivates us. But society and education suppress it in favour of logic. Instinct is still there but it's buried. Yet it is our guidance system 'par excellence' as it prompts us to go where we can find information and opportunities that are connected to the things we want to create. So, the order of work is instinct first (for direction) and logic second (to work out the detail).

Normally, however, a fleeting instinct whizzes through our mind before we have had time to properly register it, as we are focused on doing something else.

So, how do we reconnect with our instinct? Awareness is the key. This allows us to consciously register those flashes, so we can examine them. If there isn't time in the moment, then we can write them down and do it later. When instinct leads to a good decision (or avoids a bad one), we should take a moment to congratulate ourselves. If it's a biggie, I usually erupt into spontaneous whooping! But little things give me a buzz too. It's addictive – in a good way. The more positive feedback you get, the more you trust your instinct and rely on it as the powerful guidance and discernment tool it is.

But, as ever, mastery requires practice. So, it's a good idea to invent exercises to train your instinct and develop your connection to the multi-dimensional part of you. Because that's what instinct really is. It's where consciousness meets the rest of 'all that there is'.

Here are some practical exercises I use to train my instinct, based on my lifestyle. They give immediate feedback and have helped me to become more instinctive about the bigger issues in life, as well, which is the real aim. The exercises are fun and they make me smile when I get the answer right, which is most of the time now!

- The yard thermometer – I ask myself what the temperature is before looking at it as it helps me make practical decisions for the horses, such as what rugs to put on them in the stable or the field.
- The weather – I ask myself what the weather is going to do by looking at the sky, feeling the air and wind and tuning into any other natural clues, before I consult the online forecast. I do this several times a day, as the weather changes very quickly where I live. Again, it helps me make practical decisions about what I can do outside each day and the order of work, as I am outdoors most of the time working on the land, riding and looking after the animals. I am pleased to say my forecast is usually more accurate than the official one!
- The stopwatch – When I train on the static bike, I ask myself how many minutes have passed before I look at the watch. It adds interest to an otherwise dull session.
- The time – I ask myself what time it is before looking at the clock. I even do this at night when I wake up to go to the loo. Having been asleep, I feel like I've been in a different time warp but, amazingly, I am still accurate to within a few minutes.

I also dowse (with a pendulum) on practical matters such as diet, supplements and exercise for me and the animals. Dowsing is your instinct on the end of a piece of string which makes it visible. It has saved me a lot of time, money and angst over the years and has become a permanent part of my daily life.

Learning to re-connect with your instinct, however you do this, is a pre-requisite for becoming a powerful creator in your life.

What is spirituality?

6th June 2018

This is a big question but, at its simplest, here is what it means to me. Spirituality is 'everything else that there is'. It ranges from practical applications in everyday life to full-blown esoterics. My spiritual journey began in my teens with the simple question, "What more is there?" There is nothing religious or prescriptive about this. I was brought up in an orthodox religion and rebelled against it as soon as I could talk, though I now realise it inspired me to look for something else that I could relate to. I have a natural antipathy towards any religious doctrine. But there are millions of people for whom traditional religion is the conduit for discovering their spirituality, and I respect that.

We are all different and it doesn't matter how we find our connection with the divine. My path has been to develop a sense of spirituality that fits with my strong sense of individuality, and I have blended this with the notion of quantum psychology.

The more I investigated and experienced, the more I wanted to know. My spiritual connection is the main source of health, happiness and solace for me. I identify with a practical side of spirituality that has helped me to develop the tools to live a happier, healthier and altogether more satisfying life, whereas the esoteric aspect is about our connection with everything else, however we experience it.

For me, divinity is in every cell of our body. It is a multi-dimensional attribute which, as I understand it, resides in our DNA (the 90% that science says is 'junk'). I'm not going to call it God because for many, especially in the West, this evokes a concept of the divine which is male, singular and separate. I prefer to use the term 'creative source' or 'cosmic intelligence'.

So, if there is divinity in me and divinity is in everything, then there is the seed of everything in me. I am part of the 'oneness' and this means I can tap into it too. It also means I am never alone. 'I am *(all)* that I am'.

My physicality in this lifetime is my current soul expression. It's the visible tip of the iceberg of all my soul expressions. This means there is a massive storehouse of wisdom and skills I can draw upon beyond my present experience and knowledge, which arises from all of these lives – past, present and future (in our linear time construct). How could this be? Well, in a quantum state, time is described as circular, hence the idea of the 'eternal now'. So, all that has ever been, is, or will be, in terms of the wisdom of my soul, is available to me quantumly, right now. The picture is far bigger than the limited dimensions we are familiar with in our physical world. Everything is made up of energy, frequency and vibration, which is readily available to us. It's a mind-boggling resource which is there to be used.

Most of humanity accepts the notion of reincarnation. Reincarnation is driven by the engine of karma. This sets us up in any life expression to gravitate towards people and situations that allow us to acquire wisdom, depending on how we respond to them. Our responses also create learning and insight for others. Karma is a system, a multi-dimensional classroom. It's not pre-destination. We are in control of the decisions we make in life.

However, the system is changing. We are moving into a different energy paradigm, one that has been well documented in astrology (which is cosmic physics), as well as in metaphysics. This new energy is more powerful and enables us to fast-track our spiritual evolution, if we choose. One of the things we can now do, is to void our karma and become the creator of our own experiences instead. In this situation, the ability to draw on the storehouse of wisdom and talents acquired in many lifetimes (called our Akashic record) is extremely useful because it increases our ability to solve problems and become more of who we want to be.

Talking to your food

9th June 2018

'I welcome you to my biology'

I have thought a lot about what I eat over the years because it's the easiest way to support my health. Let's face it, we have direct control over what we put into our mouth! In particular, the quality, the purity, the freshness, the simplicity but also the type of food that suits us best.

I have always been extremely active, physically (in sport) and mentally (in business) and that got me thinking about how I could use food to improve my all-round performance. I also use nutritional supplements, minerals and herbs because it's difficult to get everything you need from food, as so much is processed and the quality of fresh food isn't what it used to be.

Over time, I began to notice what agreed with me and what didn't, and this enabled me to hone my diet even further. It's partly down to biology (and, quite possibly, the remembrance of what I ate in other lifetimes) but also factors such as stress, exertion, environmental toxicity and age. So, at different times of my life I have been gluten free, dairy free, sugar free or vegetarian. At other times, I have eaten a little fish or meat. I also practised a system of eating where I didn't combine protein and carbohydrate at the same meal, which improved my digestion and assimilation. Currently, my diet is largely plant-based.

However, there's something else about optimising our diet and it's very subtle. It's the idea of talking to your food in order to amplify the nutritional and energetic benefit you can get from it, over and above its face value. Through using conscious intention, I believe we can turn everything we eat into 'super' food.

I have been talking to my food most of my adult life. The words I use (out loud) are, "I welcome you into my biology and raise you to my highest vibration". I also take a moment to appreciate the taste, colour and smell of my food, as well as the journey it has made to my plate. In short, I am a conscious eater!

As I speak the words, I imagine taking in the perfect essence of the food (at peak freshness and vibrancy) and raising it to the highest biological functioning I can muster within my body. So, I am adding a quantum attribute to the food in order to enhance its nutritional value. I then use the power of thought to instruct my cells (which are 'intelligent' and know how to be healthy) to amplify the way my body uses the nutrition.

Science has proven that thought affects our biology. It has also shown that thought can change the structure of water, depending on whether the thoughts are positive or negative. And it's generally accepted that some people have 'green fingers' when it comes to gardening, which demonstrates that thought affects food. In time, I have no doubt there will be proof that thought can enhance the nutritional value of what we eat, too.

One final factor. I believe that the meal-time environment plays a part in the digestive process. If you are watching the news serving up its daily menu (pun intended) of doom, gloom, fear and all things negative, it's not likely to help you process your food. In fact, it will probably give you indigestion! Conversely, if you are having a lovely conversation, listening to music, or are fortunate, as I am, to look out onto a magnificent view, then the energy of your environment will almost certainly enhance your digestive experience.

Taking ownership of what and how you eat is a relatively easy thing to do, and the quickest way to improve your health. It's a simple recipe.

Affirmations and how to change your life

2nd July 2018

I have been using affirmations since I was a teenager. I think it started with my father who was a self-made businessman. When I was a child, he would look into the mirror before he left for work and say to himself, *"Every day in every way, I'm getting better and better"*. The idea of positive thinking and self-development wasn't exactly 'out there' in those days, so I wondered where he got it from. I discovered that this affirmation was created by a Frenchman a century earlier, who was a psychologist and pharmacist. He was light years ahead of his time and believed that much mental and physical illness was the result of the person's thinking. So, he added auto-suggestion to each prescription he dispensed and found it made a significant difference to the recovery of his customers. My father started out as a pharmacist and probably came across the Frenchman in his studies.

To me, affirmations are totally natural, and I have used them to help me change much in my life. They are even more relevant today in our fast-moving world, because whilst change brings new opportunities, it's also stressful as there are unknowns. To make successful changes, we have to think differently but changing our habits of thinking is challenging. This is where affirmations come in, as they are an effective launching pad for new intentions.

Thought is powerful. Think of the placebo effect, and cases of spontaneous remission (ie miracle recoveries). What we consistently focus our thoughts on, whether positive or negative, becomes the point of attraction for what we experience. Our thoughts are like a giant antenna. So, if we hold strong negative thoughts about our health, our body, our ability or our relationships then we are likely to manifest experiences that match them, in time. This is a slippery slope. It confirms what we fear and perpetuates a cycle of creating what we don't want, eg ill health, unhappiness and lack of abundance. But we can change all this, if we learn to work the system.

Affirmations are a powerful tool for reframing thoughts because they are purposeful statements of conscious intention. They help us to create new habits of thinking which change our point of attraction. Then, we can manifest a positive cycle of experience, which is within our control.

The rule of thumb is, make affirmations simple, positive and present tense – as if you already have 'it' or are 'it', whatever 'it' is that you want to manifest. Live 'it' and feel 'it' in your imagination because this creates a positive emotion which adds power to the words and helps you to become a match for attracting 'it' into your reality.

Here are some examples of affirmations I have used in different situations:

In times of uncertainty and challenge: "I always find my way in life and things come easily to me."

In situations of business conflict: "I am grateful for what I am learning from my colleagues and for the clarity this gives me."

When feeling isolated: "I have all the support I need and I am never alone".

When tired and jaded: "My body is healed and rejuvenated and I feel energised."

When injured: "I am in charge of my body and I instruct it to be fully balanced and healed."

When frustrated: "This puzzle has a solution and I am working the puzzle."

When unsure about what I need: "I trust myself to know what I need and how to live."

When vulnerable, afraid or threatened: "I shine my light and my light keeps me safe."

When short of money: "I am abundant in ways that surprise and delight me."

Having created your affirmations, this is how to make them work:

- Write them down and put them where you can see them, eg on stickers around the house, next to your bed, in the bathroom, or in your car.
- Say them out loud at every opportunity, because your ears pick up an energy frequency which your cellular structure understands. This frequency also amplifies the antenna of your intention in the field of potentials (which is quantum), and makes your point of attraction more powerful.
- Ensure you are balanced when you say your affirmations because this also adds power.
- Speak each word with meaning and belief.

If you practise the above and have faith in the process, the results will speak for themselves. Affirmations are an amazing tool for discovering the power to create the life you want.

How to take charge of your body and your health

30th July 2018

We have much more control over our body than is commonly thought. Most people assume we have no control except around the edges through eating a healthy diet, exercising or reducing stress. Certainly, not through using the power of thought. Our world doesn't encourage us to think this way. But if thought has energy, and if we can master our thoughts, it makes sense that we should be able to control our body, our health and our ageing process too.

How? Because the cells of our body are intelligent, and they are designed to rejuvenate. They have consciousness and they respond to what we think. If the body is diseased, then in the absence of any instructions from us (and without any other interventions), the disease will be perpetuated. Similarly, with ageing. Our biology is stuck in a default given to us by our society, as to how long we should expect to live and it's not very long. But we can instruct our body to slow down the clock, stop it, or even reduce our biological age, according to metaphysics. And I have found this to be the case in my own experience. We don't have to know the inner workings of our body to do this, either.

Taking charge of our body has two essential prerequisites. Firstly, a belief that it's possible. 'Trying' is not believing because it allows for failure. Granted, creating a big belief like "I can heal my body" doesn't happen overnight. Belief grows as you notch up a few small successes. The second prerequisite is to be balanced for as much of the time as possible and, therefore, free from negative thoughts. Balance adds power to your healing intention.

The most extreme expression of self-healing is a phenomenon called spontaneous remission. This is well-known in the medical profession. It's where a life-threatening disease vanishes (virtually overnight in many cases) and, sometimes, in the absence of any treatment (if the patient is out of options). There isn't a scientific explanation for it, though some in the medical profession are now investigating the phenomenon. Incredibly, it's been ignored hitherto!

My sense is that spontaneous remission arises in a 'do or die' situation where the person looks death in the face and choses life. The only remaining option is to take matters into their own hands and heal themselves. Their total focus and belief in that moment is the strongest message they can send to their body. The body knows how to heal itself. It is designed to self-balance (in the same way that nature self-balances).

In this moment of ultra-focus, it's likely that the cells become 100% balanced for long enough to allow the immune system to function at full capacity and eliminate the disease. 'Dis-ease' is the opposite of balance. It cannot exist if we (and, therefore, our cells) are in a balanced state. Most people accept the idea that we can think ourselves unwell (psychosomatic illness). So, why not the reverse? I know from personal experience that we can perform our own health miracles. I also know that, with awareness and practice, a state of balance (instead of imbalance) can become our norm.

Ultimately, I believe we heal ourselves. Medication, remedies and therapies all have their place and, in some cases, they are life-saving though what works for one person won't necessarily work for the next. But I suspect what's really happening is that interventions buy us time, so we can get into a better place of balance to heal ourselves. (It goes without saying that the right food and a toxic-free environment will, undoubtedly, assist our health and healing.)

What about genealogy? We are born with predispositions to develop certain types of illnesses if our immune system is severely impaired and these predispositions reflect weaknesses in our biology, some of which are hereditary. That's my understanding from metaphysics. But our genes aren't necessarily our destiny if we have a family history of chronic illness, such as cancer or heart disease. I believe we can override our biological vulnerabilities with conscious thought, by giving the cells of our body instructions for health.

If we don't take charge of our health, then a number of things might happen. For instance, we can suffer from random external toxins, including biological and chemical; we could fall prey to our thoughts and manifest the illnesses we fear; or we could become vulnerable to the subliminal messages given to us by society about what illnesses we should expect when we are old. Accepting any such narrative is tantamount to giving our body an instruction. Conversely, when we become aware of our thoughts, we can re-frame them and avoid tripping ourselves up.

Ironically, it wasn't for reasons of health that I started to train my thoughts. I began with meditation when I was a university student and continued this for about 20 years. My motivation was purely practical. Meditation allowed me to get a second wind late at night when I was struggling to stay awake and write an essay. It was equally good at relaxing my body before training. After university, it helped me to maintain focus, day-in and day-out, in a challenging professional life with few let-ups or holidays. Meditation also taught me what it felt like to be balanced and how to create this at will.

I then began to experiment with the power of thought for self-healing. I started with minor cuts and bruises and eventually progressed to an amputated finger! I was gob-smacked at what I could achieve. Similarly, I found I could give my body instructions to rejuvinate in limited hours of sleep. This technique enabled me to cope with 20 years of sleep deprivation, while I was working in London. The more results I got, the more I wanted to perfect the art of self-healing.

These days I don't meditate much – in the sense of making an appointment with myself to sit down and do it. Instead, I am focused on transforming my life into a meditation through making balance my modus operandi. Obviously, this is a work in progress. Balance, by definition, is something that changes as we are pushed and pulled by the stuff of life. So, it requires constant re-adjustment. With practice, however, the adjustments become smaller and we can regain our balance quicker. Balance promotes good health and brings peace, insight, inspiration, clarity, connection and more.

Returning to the theme of ageing. I believe we are designed to live a very long time. In fact, the scriptures tell us that some prophets lived for hundreds of years. The realization that long life is our birthright was profound for me and I have been giving my body instructions to this effect for most of my adult life. Obviously, I intend to remain in tip-top condition and appear youthful in my dotage, too!

So, how do you give yourself instructions for health? I use a combination of visualisation and words. For example, if I want to heal a cut using visualisation, I look at a perfect piece of skin close by, or on the opposite side of my body, and superimpose it in my mind's eye, over the wound. If there is blood, I imagine the blood clotting thick like treacle, or if a joint is swollen, I imagine an army of tiny people suctioning the fluid away with syringes.

If I am using words to help a specific issue, I say something like: "Attention body! The cells of my knee, arm, eye, skin (whatever the problem is) are 100% balanced and healed." Or "My eyesight is perfect and I see clearly". Alternatively, if I want to invoke general good health, then I use words like "My biology, chemistry and physics are 100% balanced." Or "My body is completely balanced and in perfect health." Basically, you can create whatever instructions you like but make them present tense, as if you already have the healing or health you want.

It may seem like a big mountain to climb but the trick is to start somewhere. Little by little, you will begin to work magic on your body and prove to yourself that you are in control of you. Claiming your healing power is an amazing rediscovery of what has always been there but forgotten through the ages.

How to regain your balance and equilibrium

8th September 2018

Nature is a master teacher. Her natural balance is beauty and tranquillity. But things happen that create frequent geopathic and elemental turmoil and, in addition, humankind has laden her with massive challenges. Yet her pull is always back towards balance, if she is given the space and the time.

So, what does it feel like to be a 'balanced' human being? For me, it's a heady mix of mental, emotional and physical factors. For instance, feeling energised and positive, grounded and strong in my core, a quiet but alert mind, a heightened state of awareness, feeling empowered and intuitive, believing the world is a great place, seeing the good in people and events, feeling gratitude and compassion. I also have a 'zinging' sensation in my ears and at the back of my head which is difficult to describe, as it's both sound and a vibration, a bit like a gentle 'hum-buzz'. I think of this as the sound of my soul, my spiritual signature, a coherence between my heart and brain, a bridge to my cellular structure, peace and connection to everything. It's a state from which anything is possible, a waking meditation which I am consciously allowing, more of the time.

And that's the point. Balance is something you allow, not create. The work is in setting yourself up to allow it but in the moment of allowance, you just are. All the 'stuff' we put on ourselves drops away and we slip into the rest of our being, the real us. We are designed to be in this space, we function best in this space and it's where we can show our magnificence. Sadly, however, at our current collective level of consciousness it's not the norm and when we lose it, we forget what it feels like and struggle to get it back. So, the most common state of being in our world is imbalance. As we evolve, this will change.

Of course, balance continually alters and if we don't make adjustments, things start to go wrong. Very quickly, we find ourself sliding down the slippery slope heading towards the abyss. We see our life as negative. We become cynical. We feel a victim of circumstances and expect the worst in everything. This turns into a self-fulfilling prophecy and perpetuates the cycle and the habit of being out of balance.

Negativity comes from fear. It's an integral part of our human nature and includes fear of failure, fear of poverty, fear of illness, disaster and more. Poor self-esteem (the feeling of being unworthy) is also rooted in fear, as are other negative emotions such as worry, intolerance, anger and hate. Overcoming fear is the biggest challenge we face individually and collectively, because it limits us. Conversely, when we are balanced, we see a much bigger picture. We also see choices and solutions.

So, how do we know when we are unbalanced? Tell-tale signs are subtle. Physical sensations are easier to spot than emotional ones. For instance, a knot in your stomach, tension, shortness of breath or poor sleep. The quicker you notice the clues, the quicker you can get back on track. And that's the rub, no-one can do it for us.

For me, the realisation that no-one can fix me but me, was a major turning point in learning how to get back into balance. I saw clearly, for the first time, that I could either wallow in my misery for hours, days, weeks, months or even years and prolong the discomfort, or I could lift off it. The bottom line is, how long are you prepared to punish yourself by staying in a bad place (no matter what caused you to be there)? It's a sobering thought.

Once you have decided enough is enough, you need a 'box of tricks' to help you, basically, a few pre-determined strategies so you don't have to invent something when you are struggling. Then you can grab a 'recovery' technique as soon as you become aware you are off balance and save yourself from crashing. Here are some quick fixes I have used over the years.

Pick a thought. Whatever you are worried about, you can always find a thought that is slightly less worrying (or a little more positive), then another and another. Repeat until your mood starts to lift. It's an incremental change in thinking that can happen in minutes, hours or days, which will help you to feel better about things and gradually restore your balance.

Distraction. Turn your attention to something completely different as soon as you notice 'negative think' creeping in. Play with your cat or dog, do something you enjoy like a hobby or exercise, list all the things you are grateful for, laugh at yourself for not noticing you lost the plot, or just plain laugh – it's healing!

Create a theme tune. Choose a song that inspires or amuses you. Sing it over and over in your head or out loud if no-one's around, to get you back in the groove.

Fantasise! Imagine yourself in a better situation and immerse yourself in the feeling of it. Embellish it. Make it as real as possible and milk it for all you are worth, until it becomes your alternative reality.

Use affirmations. Re-frame negative thoughts with affirmations. Speak them out loud and make them present tense, so you get into the idea of being or having what you want.

Find a physical trigger. Notice where you hold tension in your body eg your eyes, jaw, hands, feet, shoulders, back, stomach, and consciously release it. Physical relaxation will help you find your balance.

Or, just allow your balance to re-surface. Balance is always there (just like your heartbeat) but it gets covered up. Allow it to float back to the surface.

The more you practise re-balancing, the more proficient you will become and the quicker you will turn yourself around when the 'sh-t' hits the fan. Being balanced also means that the negative thoughts and drama of people around you won't affect you nearly as much. You'll be aware of them but the volume will be much lower.

How to help others using the power of thought

30th October 2018

For many years, I abstained from following the news. It had become sensationalist, negative, unbalanced, untrustworthy and depressing. Not much has changed. In fact, it's probably worse. But 15 years on, I have a different perspective and have begun following the news again with interest – albeit, selectively choosing my sources. I am an optimist, so I am now looking for unexpected events that have the potential to change our world, for the better. And there are many.

But there is also another reason why I am interested. I want to do something about the chaos, dysfunction, disasters and human tragedy. While I can't just hop on a plane and give support to the latest crisis in person, I can give support in a profound way from my own home, by using the energy of compassionate thought.

Anyone can benefit from compassionate thought, including family and friends in difficulty, as well as people affected by catastrophic world events such as mass shootings, forced migration, cataclysmic weather, volatile political regimes, war and whatever else is happening.

Here's what you do. Sit quietly and focus on getting yourself into balance (as if you are preparing to meditate). Let your thoughts move away from your own issues and any distractions in your environment, so that your mind is neutral but relaxed and alert. Let this peaceful state expand until you are 'humming' or 'zinging' (new word). It feels like a love-wash pouring over you and through you. Let your heart centre expand. Draw on a beautiful memory to help, if you need to.

Then, direct the feeling of 'zingingness' (balance) out into the world, either to a specific person, place or event, or simply to where it is needed. If you want to help families who have suffered bereavement as a result of a particular catastrophe, for example, imagine them smiling in the future when they are over the worst of the trauma and are ready to heal. See them finding solutions in their lives, resolution and a positive way to use the tragedy. Or, if you want to help migrants who are fleeing a war-zone, imagine them in a place where they feel safe and hopeful about starting a new life.

You don't have to invent a solution to anyone's problems, you just need to imagine them feeling better and more positive about their life in a way that's meaningful to them. Effectively, you are transmitting this intention through the frequency of your balanced energy. Those who are looking for support and inspiration will then be able to draw on this, at a time when it's difficult to find balance for themselves. Perhaps it will help them feel better, so they can see the situation from a broader perspective and make a decision that stops them becoming permanently angry or depressed. The reason you need to be balanced to send compassionate thought, is that balance adds power to what you transmit. A balanced state is free from negativity. Negativity weakens power.

How does thought travel? I suspect in the same way that you can sometimes tune into a person you have a strong connection with, when they are a long way away. I imagine that compassionate thought travels along some sort of 'cosmic super-highway' to its destination.

And that's not all. Coherent group thought is even more powerful. Maybe this is how some of the 'wild card' events in history have happened, events which were unexpected and beyond imagination such as the fall of the Berlin Wall? Perhaps enough people around the world organized their thought and prayers collectively to create a peaceful outcome to the Cold War? Today, thousands of people are doing the same for a variety of causes including peace in the Middle East and elsewhere. Science is interested too, after noticing a change in the earth's magnetic field during the global wave of compassion that followed 9/11, and the Japanese tsunami. So, I have no doubt that what is controversial today will be the science of tomorrow.

Consciously creating the life you want

10ᵗʰ December 2018

Using conscious thought to create the life you want and become the master of your own health, abundance, joy and so much more is a very big subject. It's actually the synthesis of some of my other writings on themes such as the power of thought, narrating your life, affirmations, taking charge of your health, energising your food, living in balance and using compassionate thought to help others. So, I will do my best to put it all together here.

Let's start with the idea that in order to develop your thought into a powerful tool capable of conscious manifestation, you first have to become aware of what you think, as this influences what you say, how you behave, your beliefs about yourself and others and, eventually, what you experience. Being aware of your thoughts is the start of living consciously.

Thought has energy. It is part of our consciousness and this has a known effect on our biology and the world around us. It's a system which delivers what we are strongly focused on, whether it's positive or negative, what we want or what we don't want. Essentially, our thoughts and beliefs make up an energy signature which magnetises to us the things that match our focus. They are drawn from a quantum soup of potentials called the 'field' which we are energetically entangled with. Difficult as it is, changing our thinking is the most effective way to change our reality.

From very early on in life, I believed it was possible to make things happen. Initially, sport demonstrated to me that I could use my mind to master my body, through a combination of dogged determination, positive intention and visualisation. Later on, business became my working laboratory to explore the process of manifestation.

Fast forward 40 years and I have continued to hone the power of thought, though I am under no illusion that this is a lifetime's work (and many more). Nonetheless, I can see tangible evidence of my efforts, including robust health, fitness, vitality, a slowing of the ageing process, abundance, a balanced lifestyle, passion-led work, solutions and a sense of peace. This is the 'designer' reality I have created for myself.

Knowing I am in charge of my body and my life has completely changed my outlook and made worry and stress largely a thing of the past – what a lot of time, angst and unhappiness that saves! Note, I used the word 'knowing'. This is different to 'believing'. It's the certainty you have when you look down your arm and know your hand is at the end of it. When I am emotionally balanced and I feel good about myself, I absolutely know that the cells of my body are balanced, and dis-ease cannot exist in a balanced state.

At a practical level, I give instructions to my body on a daily basis. I tell my biology (out loud) to be 100% balanced, also my chemistry, hormones, physiology, emotions and my subtle energy field too. If I have injuries, I give my body instructions to mend, and I have been amazed, time and again, at the speed of healing and recovery.

At some level, I feel there is even more and we should be able to create immediate results in our body. Proof that this is possible is found in the cases of spontaneous remission which doctors see occasionally. It's where a patient with a terminal illness achieves full recovery, sometimes, in hours or days.

From studying metaphysics, I understand that our DNA is linked to consciousness. As our consciousness expands, DNA becomes more efficient, enabling us to access greater functionality which is otherwise hidden. This means we become more intuitive, more aware of our connection with each other and our divinity, more powerful at healing ourselves and others, and wiser (through a remembrance of experiences and talents gained in other lifetimes). These attributes are linked to the multi-dimensional part of our DNA – the 90% scientists call junk.

How does this relate to health? Well, as our consciousness evolves, I expect we'll become so attuned to our bodies that we will know immediately if anything is wrong and what to do about it. After all, many species below us in the evolutionary chain know what to eat to heal themselves and some can even re-grow parts of their body. So, surely, we, as the most advanced species on the planet, should be able to do this and more?

I also believe we are built to regenerate and live a very long time. When I stumbled across this notion in my early twenties, it was a lightbulb moment. I knew, there and then, that our bodies are capable of so much more. Perhaps high-functioning DNA was the secret of some biblical prophets and leaders who purportedly lived super-long lives? Maybe it's how miracles were performed? A number of more recent spiritual masters have also been able to perform miracles, and the recurring message from all of them, is that we are made of the same stuff and what they can do, we can do!

However, given my relatively modest DNA functionality at the present time, I should mention that, in addition to talking to my cells and working on maintaining a state of balance, I also take practical measures to support my health and well-being. I trust my instinct to guide me to what I need to know including what foods are best for me and the ones to avoid, any dietary supplements I need, herbs, homeopathic and other naturopathic remedies that suit me, and which exercise is most appropriate. To make it easier, I dowse these things with a pendulum, which is my instinct on the end of a piece of string.

So, back to the main question – *how do you use thought to create the life you want?* I will talk you through the process I use (still a work in progress) which is relatively simple, though that's not to say it's easy. It takes practice and you need to be adept at noticing what you think and re-framing any negative thoughts.

To energise something new (ie give a spark of life to your manifestation), the first step is to fantasise about it. Imagine what you want to bring into your life so vividly that you can almost reach out and touch it. Spend time with it in your imagination, and embellish it. This adds power to the process of creation. Don't get hung up on the detail because there are lots of ways something can come into being which are beyond what you know or have experienced. If you get too fixed on one idea, you might miss something that's even better! So, imagine what the thing, person, place, situation or experience will feel like (as opposed to look like) and immerse yourself in it through all your senses. Banish any doubts that creep in, as they will weaken your power to manifest and slow or stop the process.

Now that you have breathed life into your creation, the next step is to 'own it' as *real* in your future. In metaphysics, time is considered to be circular – past, present and future are one and on the same circuitous track, with no beginning and no end. So, what you have manifested with your thought now exists on the track. You just can't see it yet because, in our linear world, the future is in front of you.

The final step is to be patient and stay balanced so that your instinct can guide you to your creation (or it to you), through a process of synchronicity, which is the engine of manifestation. These concepts are impossible to fully grasp as they are outside our limited dimensional 'reality'. The best we can do is to get a sense of them and take a leap of faith. We don't have to know exactly how it works. Proof that it does, is sufficient.

Timing is the other factor. Synchronicity is a collision of what you and others are manifesting in the field of potentials, which we are all entangled with energetically. It's a bit like a Rubik's Cube – lots of configurations must line up before it clicks into place and the puzzle is solved. However, because we can change our minds about what we want at any time, if one link in the chain falls away, it changes everything and another chain has to be created. This is why timing is of the essence and patience is key. Granted, it's a simplistic way of describing something that's inexplicable. Obviously, it's much bigger and grander than this.

By the time you have created what you want, it probably won't seem as incredible as when you conceived it. You will have normalised the idea through fantasising about it and expecting it. Nonetheless, it's important to recognize it came from *your* creative process and that self-congratulations are due. I also thank the 'invisible helping hand' that supported me, synchronically. This is the leading edge of consciousness and it's a game changer.

Dowsing with a pendulum – the ultimate 'smart' device

12th March 2019

Dowsing with a pendulum is an amazing tool and one that I have been using for over 30 years. Basically, it's your instinct on the end of a piece of string, with the massive advantage that it's visible. It's the same principle as muscle-testing in Kinesiology, which is a diagnostic tool that asks the all-knowing part of your body (your 'innate') what the problem (and the remedy) is. Given that instinct is our best guidance, dowsing is very handy and it has saved me a huge amount of time and effort, not to mention money. Instinct is fleeting and easily missed. But dowsing provides a way to see it, question it, ponder it and act on it.

The technique is remarkably simple, though you have to trust it and be open-minded about the answers. Lack of trust (through fear or expectation) is likely to affect the answer. Obviously, trust grows over time with positive feedback, so it's a matter of sticking with it to gain experience and improve your confidence. You also need to be balanced when you dowse. If you are not, then the simple rule is, don't dowse.

I use a plastic pendulum as it's an inert material and doesn't hold any energy of its own, which might influence the answer. But many people dowse with a crystal. That's fine – just affirm it will serve your highest good. The piece of cotton I attach to my pendulum is about 6 inches long, which is a comfortable length to hold and dowse with. But whatever you are using, the important thing is that once you are holding it between your thumb and forefinger, the ideal length from there to the pendulum is about 3 inches.

Where do you start? The easiest exercise to start with is to ask your pendulum to give you a 'yes' and 'no' direction, so that you can use it to answer simple questions. Draw a large cross on a piece of paper and another cross dissecting it. This gives you four axes. Now, you can ask your pendulum which axis is 'yes' and which is 'no'. It won't be the same for everyone.

Set your pendulum moving gently in a small, slow, clockwise, circular motion just above the page. Then, beginning at the top of your diagram, move the pendulum (maintaining this gentle motion) around the axes, whilst keeping the question in mind, "Show me my yes line" which will either be the vertical line, the horizontal one, or one of the two lines in-between.

As you move clockwise around the perimeter of the diagram, be sensitive to the pendulum pushing or pulling you gently towards one line or another. It will probably look as if it's trying to change from swinging in a circular motion to swinging in a straight line, when you reach your 'yes' line. Check by pushing the pendulum a little to the left and a little to the right of where you think it wants to be, and feel if there is any resistance. It's very subtle and you'll have to play around with it until you get the idea. There is no need to go all the way around the circle if the pendulum is clear about taking you towards a particular line.

Repeat the exercise to find your 'no' line. Chances are, the two are opposite each another. It's important to keep your mind blank after you've asked the question. If you struggle to do this, keep repeating the question (in your head, or out loud) so your mind stays neutral.

The next exercise is to ask some simple questions for a 'yes' or 'no' answer, either dowsing on your diagram or, for convenience, superimposing the 'yes' and 'no' axes visually onto the palm of your hand, and dowsing over that. In the latter case, set your pendulum onto a small, slow circle over your palm and let it take you to your 'yes' or 'no' axis to answer the question.

A word of caution! Dowsing isn't suitable for questions which are emotionally charged, as your emotions are likely to influence the answer. It works best for practical issues. I use it for things like the horses' daily feed and exercise regimes, any issues with their health, treatments and remedies. And the same sorts of things for me. However, these questions are more complex than a simple 'yes' or 'no' answer and require a different approach.

Firstly, make your question as clear and precise as possible. If it's a subject I don't know much about, I do some research to help me frame the question. Sometimes, several rounds of research and dowsing are necessary to narrow down the options. At each stage, write down the options in a list format and hold the question in mind, eg "Which is the best option for x, y, z?". Put the pendulum onto a small, slow circle and dowse down the list to see which item it gravitates towards and wait for it to change from a circle into a horizontal line. Then nudge the pendulum up and down a little to see if there is any resistance, so you are sure of the answer it is taking you to.

Charts as opposed to lists work better in some situations. For instance, you can draw a circle and divide it into segments to dowse for essential oils, flower remedies, foods or types of exercise. If there are lots of items, you can make it easier by dividing the circle into quarters. Ask your pendulum which quarter the answer is in and dowse over the segments in that quarter.

Sometimes, the answer might be more than one thing, if it's a complicated issue such as diet. So, make a chart for numbers (or use the fingers of your hand) and ask how many things you need to know. Then dowse down your list of options for the first one and the second one etc. At other times, it might be helpful to know the degree to which something is the answer. So, draw a straight line and mark it 1-10 (representing 10% – 100%) and dowse on that. You can also make charts for days of the week and months of the year. The possibilities are endless.

The great thing is that you don't need to spend years studying everything you need to know in order to stay fit and well and make practical decisions in your daily life. A pendulum is the ultimate 'smart' device. It enables you to tune into a higher, multi-dimensional wisdom and go straight to the answers.

Connecting with nature

13th April 2019

At one with nature

'Connecting with nature' is a well-used expression but what does it really mean? One thing is certain, it means different things to different people. So, I will talk from my own experience which came about primarily from a radical change of lifestyle, from 'city professional' to 'semi-feral'.

Connecting with nature isn't the same as being in nature whilst you are doing something else. I have spent a lot of time outdoors over the years, doing sport. But I wasn't paying much attention to the natural world other than to the weather, which was often an additional and unwelcome challenge. However, I did develop a strong connection with my animals (which are part of nature, of course) and became instinctively aware of their needs. I could also communicate with them through body language and telepathy, both of which are normal for animals.

It was only when I moved to Wales and began my rewilding experience, living remotely with my animals, in solitude, in an area of dramatic weather, that things changed. First of all, the wall-to-wall beauty was impossible to ignore. Not only breathtaking scenery but ever-changing light, the personality of the sky, the sunset and the stars. I ogled at the sheer magnitude of living art all around me.

Necessity, however, was the catalyst for me to connect to the elements. I was immersed in them with the animals, living high up in a meandering valley which amplified the worst of the weather, bringing rain of biblical proportions, gales and snow. It was, therefore, a matter of safety for all of us and the ancient farmhouse, that I tuned into the weather.

The forecast wasn't always reliable, so I began sensing the mood of the weather to get a feel for when extreme conditions were on the way, in order to get provisions and do the necessary preparations to keep us all safe. It gave me the heads-up on when not to leave the premises, when it was unsafe to ride (as all routes were uphill, where the weather was even worse), how to prioritise maintenance and repairs, when the fields would be too wet for grazing or, conversely, when there was a window of opportunity to work on the land. There was also the issue of what clothes the horses should wear in and out of their stables. So, I would stand in the yard and study the sky, feel the air and the wind and ask intuitively for an indication of what to expect.

I also started to notice more detail in the natural world. When eating al fresco, I would watch the birds, butterflies and bees going about their business and cheeky squirrels stealing fallen pears from the tree. I would notice shafts of light piercing the clouds, spring buds popping up or the leaves changing colour in the autumn. I would listen to the sound of the wind and the gurgling stream, enjoy the warmth of the sun and watch the feral cats hunting and playing. I even met a polecat that lived under the floorboards in the barn and a hedgehog family which was hibernating in an old dog kennel in the garden. I was in my own private cinema watching the movie of life. The more I noticed, the more nature revealed herself to me and I realised I was just one of the many residents living at my property, merely the guardian of what I inhabited, as you can't own nature.

The light was continually astonishing. Rainbows appeared after a storm for a few brief seconds, as if just for me, then another and another. I have never seen so many. I would find myself in the right place at the right time to witness a jaw-dropping sunset morphing into endless shades of exquisiteness every time I looked up. Eventually, I concluded that the light responded to me, through my awareness of it. I wanted to see it and it appeared. I appreciated it and it revealed more of itself. It was a beautiful symbiotic relationship with nature which showed me we are connected with everything, including the elements, and that everything is 'intelligent'.

I later experimented with another level of connection by asking pieces and parts of nature for their wise messages. The moon, for instance, which I frequently observed from the window seat in my bedroom, told me, "Be still and shine your light bright as I do." The elderly pear tree in the garden whispered, "Reach into the roots of your wisdom for answers".

Continuing the theme of communication, I have always believed it's possible to influence the local weather (at least a little) and, over the years, I asked for co-operation when I needed it. Sometimes, my requests took the form of poems, for the right hay-making weather, for instance. By and large, the elements obliged me for just the right amount of time.

When rewilding in Wales, my most frequent requests were for safety and not to have more weather than I could cope with on my own with the animals, the property and the land. From studying all things metaphysical, I came to understand that the elements can co-operate with us when we ask with a pure intention. Small detours of wind and rain are possible as long as it doesn't create a catastrophic situation nearby, as local weather is part of a larger weather system and can't simply disappear.

I believe the Gaia system (including the earth, sky, light, fauna, flora, elements and stars) is conscious and benevolent. After all, how could it not be when the trees exhale the oxygen we need to breathe? You may not think Gaia is on our side when you read about major climate events such as earthquakes, volcanic eruptions, wildfires and tsunamis. But contrary to popular opinion, there are many experts who believe we are in a natural cycle, one that has occurred before where current weather volatility is the transition into a cooling phase which is preceded by a warming. One possible reason could be to refresh the oceans, which are vital for our survival. Because the planet is a closed system, temperature change might be the only way to achieve this.

The separate matter of man-made toxins polluting the air, the water and the environment, which are killing us and the planet, is not in doubt. But it doesn't necessarily mean, that this is the cause of catastrophic climate events and a rise in temperature. We need to remain open to all possibilities and be aware of vested interests that stifle debate. In any event, detoxing our world is within our control and it's imperative we find the collective will and the means to do this.

Gaia is our biological parent. The earth and the elements collaborated to create the spark of life which gave birth to humanity. So, we are connected with nature through our DNA. There is a saying, "If you love Gaia, you love yourself and if you love yourself you love Gaia".

Such simple awareness has the power to change our world and inspire natural solutions to some of the biggest questions of our time including food production, clean water, energy and sustainability. There is 'magic' to be discovered through our connection with nature.

Quantumness

28th June 2019

Ready to run. Four times the benefit please!

'Quantum' is an increasingly popular term but it's confusing to the majority of us who are not scientists. In science, quantum physics is the study of energy at the smallest levels of matter, namely, sub-atomic particles where the laws of physics appear to be different to those of larger matter. However, in metaphysics (which is the study of reality and the relationship between mind and matter), 'quantum' is thought of as a paradigm outside the world we know, basically, beyond the laws of physics. Yet metaphysics is science too – we just haven't discovered how it all works. But when we do, I believe there will be a confluence of science and spirituality, resulting in a massive shift in human consciousness. In the here and now, though, I want to talk about what 'quantum' means to me and how I use it in practical ways in my life.

Let's start with time. In my experience, time is flexible. When I look back at the most intense part of my business life, I am astonished at what I crammed into each day for the best part of 35 years, given the sheer mountain of work involved in building several businesses from scratch, whilst simultaneously competing in sport at international level, developing my spiritual awareness, caring for my animals and all the other stuff of life. I admit I was in perpetual motion but it took more than that. I was conscious of making time fit the task, through visualisation and affirmations. I used the power of thought to leverage my productivity and effectiveness in a quantum sort of way, beyond what should have been possible.

I also manipulated time on my commute to London for many years. The journey was at least two hours each way and getting to the station in the morning was often hazardous, especially when I found myself behind slow-moving farm vehicles on small country lanes. Trains weren't frequent from such a rural location, so arriving at the station on time was crucial.

My strategy, when I got held up, was to replace anxiety with an image of time stretching like an elastic band. The end point was fixed (ie the time the train pulled into the station) but between where I was on my journey and the end point, I visualised the elastic band of time being infinitely stretchy. And it worked. Even when I arrived with minutes to spare and couldn't immediately find a parking place, or discovered the ticket machine wasn't working, or had to sprint to the platform with all my bags, I never missed a train. Applying the same sort of principle to my life now (on car journeys), I intend for perfect timing which also implies safety and I usually arrive within minutes of my expected time, in spite of hold-ups.

I use the idea of quantumness in fitness training, too. At the start of each session, I tell my body, "It's easy" (especially when I know it will hurt) and the pain is never quite as bad. I also instruct my body to get quadruple the fitness from each session. (Initially, I was less ambitious and just asked for double!) This means I do the minimum training in the shortest time for the maximum benefit, and maintain my ideal fitness on fewer sessions than I would expect. I use the same principle for lifting heavy objects (unavoidable when living alone and working with horses). Just saying the word 'quantum' as I lift, I am able to amplify my strength and lift without straining.

Then there is health. I instruct the cells of my body to be balanced, so I don't get ill and to heal injuries much more quickly, too. I also give instructions to my body to 'youth' ie slow the ageing process, and I talk to my food to maximise its nutritional value. The more you tap into quantumness, the more you can leverage your effectiveness. It's not in any textbook and you can't download an instruction manual. But just like driving your car, you can turn it on without knowing how the engine works!

Final Words

As you will know by now, the material in this book was written over a 20-year period. It then took time to put it together and update. This was done following the conclusion of my rewilding experience. After leaving Wales, I had intended to start a new life abroad, but global events precluded this. So, instead, I embarked on a solo 'circumnavigation' of the British Isles aboard a shiny new set of wheels, to see the marvellous coastline.

I was in uncharted territory, in every respect. Finally, I was free from the responsibilities and commitments that had sustained a life of perpetual motion and I had a blank canvas to reinvent myself yet again. It was a major transformation and more challenging than I expected. I knew in my mind that I had to cut loose, but I underestimated the process of catchup for the rest of me – my body, my emotions and patterns of behaviour. Ironically, it brought me right back to what you have just read in this book.

Re-visiting the material couldn't have been more timely. It revealed yet another layer of 'the ultimate relationship', which is never-ending and constantly surprising. Perhaps I will write about it in the future, from somewhere else in the world? For now, though, I am enjoying a nomadic existence, which feels strangely familiar – I suspect I have done it before but perhaps with camels, last time!

To give you a context for the final editing of the book, which was done on board 'the ship' in so many beautiful locations, I have created a photo gallery of my UK tour. Scan the QR code to view on my website, where you can also follow my writings and podcasts. I hope my book helps you to become a grander version of you and create more of the life you want. I would love to hear your story.

About Fiona Price

At the age of 28, Fiona founded a firm of Independent Financial Advisers in London, to pioneer financial advice for women, and was heralded as 'The first woman of finance' by *Harpers & Queen*. Over a period of 17 years (from 1988), she built the business into one of the most respected and high-profile firms of advisers in the UK. During this time, Fiona frequently contributed to the media and was profiled in 8 books on women entrepreneurs. She won three national businesswomen's awards and appeared in the *Top 100 List of Power and Influence in Financial Services* in 2003 and 2004. Whilst building her business, Fiona also set up a non-profit network for women financial advisers.

Later, Fiona held a variety of non-executive directorships, as well as advisory roles, including one with a micro-finance charity which helped women in the developing world to start their own businesses, as a means of escaping poverty. She was 'Women's Champion' on the Government's Small Business Council and also mentored fellow businesswomen.

In 2007, Fiona moved into broadcast and became an internet video pioneer. Her website, 'Diva-Biz', published video interviews with high profile businesswomen, telling their stories and showcasing women's leadership style. After that, she was asked to head up a fledgling SKY channel called *Horse & Country TV*, where she was able to combine her passion for horses and her love of business.

Next, Fiona launched an equestrian video website called 'Horse Hero', also at the cutting edge of web development. This time, pioneering a subscription business model. Fiona filmed top professionals and Olympic riders training and caring for their horses at home and also followed them behind the scenes at major competitions. She made over 1200 videos and the site had a cult following.

Then came a reclusive period where Fiona lived remotely on a smallholding in the Welsh hills, looking after her animals and the land. She narrated her semi-feral lifestyle on a website called 'Rewilding in Wales'.

Prior to starting work, Fiona spent a year in Australia teaching at Timbertop School, the Australian equivalent to Gordonstoun. On her return to the UK, she did a degree in Psychology, followed by an MBA. Sport has also featured strongly in Fiona's life and she has competed in two sports at international level, rowing and the equestrian sport of endurance.

Fiona says, "Early on I realised that the ultimate relationship is the one with yourself. How you manage yourself is key to being the best version of you and creating the life experiences you want, rather than reacting to random events. Of course, it is easier said than done because the life-long habits of thinking and doing trip us up. But with awareness and practice, I have learned it is possible to change the mindsets that hinder us and re-focus our thoughts to become a conscious creator in our life."

She continues, "A sense of spirituality has played an important part in my life because it allowed me to see the bigger picture when dealing with everyday issues. It has also enabled me to better understand the world. My version of spirituality is practical. It is about engaging the quantum (or multi-dimensional) part of you in order to be healthier, happier, more abundant, more inspired and more of whatever you want, by taking control of your thoughts, your body and your life. Consciousness affects matter. We know this. One day, I believe there will be explanations for everything that is currently invisible and esoteric."

Connect with Fiona at www.theultimaterelationship.co.uk